"Seems everybody knows how to cook - they take it so seriously and are so smart - everyone, that is, but me! I'm so ~~intimidated~~, ~~intigrated~~, ~~interpretated~~, scared to death by words like stock, cilantro, braise. (Me, who looked for lemon zest next to vanilla in the spice section at the grocery. Me, who couldn't find etouffee in the dictionary because I was looking under "A".) Robin Copper Benzlé lightens up the subject of cooking. She grants permission to be less than a know-it-all in the kitchen and uses familiar terms like egg whites and white wine. I'm pulling the shoulder pads out of my rummage sale to use as hot pads. There's hope for me!"

—Margaret Noonan Blaum
Executive Assistant to Chef Paul Prudhomme

COOKING
WITH
HUMOR
a unique recipe collection

OTHER BOOKS BY ROBIN COPPER BENZLÉ:

COOKING WITH HUMOR

a unique recipe collection
by Robin Copper Benzlé

Artwork by George Kocar

VANTINE
PUBLISHING COMPANY

BAY VILLAGE, OHIO

PUBLISHER'S CATALOGING IN PUBLICATION
   (PREPARED BY QUALITY BOOKS INC.)

BENZLÉ, ROBIN COPPER, 1950-
   COOKING WITH HUMOR: A UNIQUE RECIPE COLLECTION/
ROBIN COPPER BENZLÉ. - -
   p. cm.
   ISBN 0-9629398-4-6

   1. COOKERY.   I. TITLE

TX715   641.5

                                    91-90952

THE INFORMATION CONTAINED IN THIS BOOK IS NOT INTENDED TO SLIGHT ANY PERSONS OR ORGANIZATIONS AND IS WRITTEN PURELY IN THE INTEREST OF HUMOR. IF ANYONE IS OFFENDED, LIGHTEN UP AND GET A LIFE.

PRINTED IN THE UNITED STATES OF AMERICA

FIRST PRINTING SEPTEMBER 1991
SECOND PRINTING MARCH 1992

DEDICATED TO BAILEY AND ERIN - I LOVE YOU
EVEN MORE THAN CHOCOLATE.

CONTENTS

CONTENTS

CONTENTS

SWEETS:

OTHER:

GREAT COMBINATIONS:

CONTENTS

ACKNOWLEDGMENTS

A MILLION THANKS TO:

ERIC BENZLÉ
MARY EITZEN
BRUCE BURTON
ERIC BENZLÉ
CONNIE BOZELL
KARL GROSS
BRUCE BURTON
ERIC BENZLÉ
ERIC BENZLÉ
ED NORRIS
JILL BATTERSHELL
HEATHER COPPER
ERIC BENZLÉ
JOHN PEREZ
JULIA CHILD
RICK COOPER

AND LAST BUT NOT LEAST, ERIC BENZLÉ

INTRODUCTION

SOMETIMES I LOVE TO COOK. MY KITCHEN BECOMES MY CHEMISTRY LAB AND I BECOME THE MAD SCIENTIST, EXPERIMENTING WITH VARIOUS TASTES AND TEXTURES. OCCASIONALLY, I LIKE TO TRY COMPLICATED GOURMET RECIPES; THE KIND WITH 89 INGREDIENTS THAT FINDS YOU IN IMPORTED FOOD STORES, SEARCHING DUSTY SHELVES FOR SPICES YOU CAN'T EVEN PRONOUNCE - THE KIND THAT TAKES 3 DAYS TO PREPARE - THE KIND THAT WHEN SERVED, FEELS LIKE YOU ARE THROWING THE SHEET OFF OF A MASTERPIECE.

SOMETIMES I HATE TO COOK. ON THOSE OCCASIONS, NOTHING SOUNDS MORE APPEALING THAN A BOILED WEINER ROLLING AROUND ON A PAPER PLATE. OR A MEDIUM ANCHOVY PIZZA, DELIVERED.

ALL IN ALL, COOKING HAS BEEN A CREATIVE OUTLET FOR ME THAT SEES NO BOUNDS. IT IS AN ART THAT CAN BE LEARNED FROM FOR A LIFETIME. MY OTHER FAVORITE THING IN LIFE IS LAUGHTER. **COOKING WITH HUMOR** IS AN ATTEMPT TO COMBINE THESE TWO ARTS, AND SPEAKING OF ART, I DECIDED TO HAVE EACH RECIPE ARTISTICALLY INTERPRETED BY THE ABSTRACT MIND OF GEORGE KOCAR.

ALTHOUGH NOT INTENDED AS AN INTERNATIONAL COOKBOOK, THE RECIPES (PARTY FOOD, MAIN COURSES, SIDE DISHES, AND SWEETS) DABBLE WITH THE FLAVORS OF FRANCE, CHINA, GERMANY, ITALY, JAPAN, MEXICO, AFRICA, POLAND, THE CARIBBEAN, HUNGARY, ENGLAND, THE PHILLIPINES, AND ALL OVER AMERICA.

WITH PLEASURE, I PRESENT TO YOU 100 OF MY FAVORITE RECIPES. SO, SIFT THROUGH THE FUNNY STUFF, GET DOWN TO SOME SERIOUS COOKING, AND ABOVE ALL, ENJOY YOURSELF IN THE KITCHEN.

Robin Copper Bandza

KEY:
- tsp. = TEASPOON
- T. = TABLESPOON
- C. = CUP
- oz. = OUNCE
- lb. = LIB

NOTE: SERVINGS ARE GENEROUS.

5 INGREDIENTS FOR A BETTER PARTY

1. **LABEL YOUR HORS D'OEUVRES.** MAKE PLACECARD-TYPE SIGNS AND LABEL ALL BUT THE OBVIOUS. (ONE TIME I BIT INTO A VANILLA NOUGAT BALL ROLLED IN CHOPPED PECANS. OR SO I THOUGHT. IT WAS ACTUALLY SOME SORT OF CREAM CHEESE THING ROLLED IN FAKE BACON CHIPS. I THINK.)

*2. **OFFER A VARIETY OF FOODS.** SERVE A LITTLE MEAT, A LITTLE POULTRY, A LITTLE FISH, A LITTLE CHEESE, A LITTLE VEGETABLE, A LITTLE SWEET. OFFER SOMETHING CRUNCHY, SOMETHING SOFT, SOMETHING RICH, SOMETHING LIGHT, SOMETHING WARM, SOMETHING COLD, SOMETHING SPICY, SOMETHING MILD, SOMETHING ELEGANT, SOMETHING WHIMSICAL, SOMETHING BORROWED, SOMETHING BLUE.

3. **DECORATE FOOD WITH FLOWERS.** UNLESS YOU HAVE TIME TO CARVE SWANS OUT OF RADISHES, PURCHASE A BUNCH OR TWO OF ASSORTED CUT FLOWERS, SNIP THE FLOWER HEADS OFF, WASH GENTLY UNDER COOL WATER, AND PLACE RANDOMLY ON HORS D'OEUVRE TRAYS.

4. **INVITE INTERESTING PEOPLE.** DON'T KEEP INVITING THE SAME OLD CROWD. CHANGE YOUR GUEST LIST EACH TIME TO INCLUDE A FEW FRESH FACES. INVITE SOMEONE WHO WOULD NEVER EXPECT AN INVITATION.

5. **HAVE MUSIC.** IT SETS THE STAGE FOR A GOOD PARTY AND PROMOTES CONVERSATION. I WORRY MORE ABOUT THE MUSIC SYSTEM BREAKING DOWN THAN THE FOOD BURNING.

* LOOK IN THE **SWEETS** SECTION, STARTING ON PAGE 111 FOR ADDITIONAL PARTY OFFERINGS.

10 THINGS NEVER TO SERVE AT A PARTY

1. ONE OF THOSE ROUND PUMPERNICKEL LOAVES HOLLOWED OUT WITH SPINACH DIP IN THE MIDDLE.

2. PLAIN CREAM CHEESE CANAPÉS WITH OLIVE SLICES ON TOP.

3. LEFTOVER PIZZA CUT UP INTO LITTLE SQUARES.

4. A BOWL OF POTATO CHIPS.

5. PROCESSED CHEESE FOOD SQUARES WITH TOOTHPICKS.

6. COCKTAIL WEINERS WITH KETCHUP DIP.

7. PORK TARTARE.

8. EGGS EN GELÉE.

9. TOMATO ASPIC ON TOAST POINTS.

10. ANYTHING OUT OF A JAR MARKED "MADE IN PERSIA".

NEWLYWED NUTS

  1   C. PECAN OR WALNUT HALVES
  1/4 C. SUGAR
  1   T. CINNAMON
  1/2 tsp. NUTMEG
  1   EGG WHITE, SLIGHTLY BEATEN

GO INTO THE KITCHEN. IF IT IS DARK, TURN THE LIGHTS ON. PREHEAT OVEN TO 300° (TO TURN OVEN ON, LOOK AT THE FRONT OF THE UNIT. LOCATE THE TEMPERATURE CONTROL KNOB. TURN IT UNTIL THE MARK LINES UP WITH THE NUMBER 300.)

MEASURE NUTS IN A CHIPPED COFFEE MUG (REMOVE COFFEE FIRST) AND PUT IN MEDIUM BOWL (BORROW BOWL FROM A NEIGHBOR). ADD SUGAR, CINNAMON, AND NUTMEG. THESE INGREDIENTS CAN BE PURCHASED AT A GROCERY STORE. CALL YOUR MOTHER TO FIND OUT HOW TO SEPARATE THE EGG WHITE FROM THE EGG YOLK AND ADD BEATEN EGG WHITE TO NUT MIXTURE.

SPREAD MIXTURE ON BUTTERED COOKIE SHEET. IF YOU DON'T HAVE A COOKIE SHEET, USE AN OVEN-PROOF MAKE-UP TRAY. BAKE 30 MINUTES. YOU SHOULD HAVE ENOUGH TIME FOR A QUICKIE.

USE A POT HOLDER WHEN REMOVING TRAY FROM OVEN. IF YOU DON'T HAVE A POT HOLDER, USE AN EXTRA-HEAVY SHOULDER PAD. TURN OVEN CONTROL KNOB TO "OFF."

LET NUTS COOL AND BREAK INTO PIECES. PLACE IN CEREAL BOWL. TURN KITCHEN LIGHT OUT. SERVE.

WASH DISHES IN A FEW DAYS.

KOCAR

GORP (gôrp) n. ANY COMBINATION OF THREE OR MORE MUNCHIES OF SIMILAR SIZES. FOUND PRIMARILY ON COFFEE TABLES DURING PARTIES. CONSUMED BY NORTH AMERICAN HUMANOIDS.

SUGGESTIONS:

1. CASHEWS, CHOCOLATE-COVERED RAISINS, AND SMALL PRETZELS OR PRETZEL STICKS, OR

2. MACADAMIA NUTS, CHUNKS OF WHITE CHOCOLATE, PRETZEL RINGS, AND MUSCAT RAISINS, OR

3. CHOCOLATE-COVERED PEANUTS, DRIED BANANA CHIPS, AND CORN CHIPS, OR

4. SHELLED JUMBO PISTACHIO NUTS, SESAME CHIPS, AND CHUNKS OF DARK CHOCOLATE.

MALGORP (mălgôrp) n. ANY INCOMPATIBLE COMBINATION OF THREE OR MORE MUNCHIES OF UNSIMILAR SIZES. ORIGIN UNKNOWN. CONSUMED MOSTLY BY MENSA MEMBERS.

SUGGESTIONS:

1. WHOLE WATERMELONS, RICE KRISPIES, AND MUSHROOM CAPS, OR

2. BLEU CHEESE CHUNKS, WHOLE GARLIC CLOVES, AND SPICED GUMDROPS, OR

3. MINIATURE MARSHMALLOWS, SWEET GHERKINS, AND ANCHOVY FILLETS, OR

4. FRESH STRAWBERRIES, BOILED OKRA, AND PICKLED PIG'S FEET.

MAKES ABOUT 28

DOWN:

2 ___ DAYS OF CHRISTMAS
3 DUO DECIMAL
5 CUBE
8 COCOA SEED PRODUCT
10 I THINK I ___
12 BRINED
14 ___ THE MOOD
15 STEAMER
19 SMALL WEIGHT (PL.)
20 ONION SKIN
21 EARLIEST
23 ___ GOLDEN POND
25 ___ HOUSE
26 WILLIE WONKA AND THE ___ FACTORY
28 PARAFIN
31 SMALL MONEY (PL.)

ANSWERS ON P.156

ACROSS:

1 DISSOLVE
4 1/16 POUND
6 MINUTELY
7 PARCEL
9 AVOIRDUPOIS
11 GOOBERS
13 POKER ___ (PL.)
16 ROB ROY
17 ___-CROSS
18 DRUMBEAT
22 GIVE THE GREEN LIGHT
24 ___ LITTLE INDIANS
27 ___ DA GADDA DA VIDA
29 FREEZE
30 CIGAR-SHAPED MUNCHIES (2 WDS.)
32 AT THAT TIME
33 ___ A PINCH

CRACKERS DON'T GROW IN BOXES
(BUT THERE IS A SANTA CLAUS)

HOMEMADE WALNUT-MALT CRACKERS SERVED WITH WARM
BRIE CHEESE AND ALMONDS.

SERVES ABOUT 15-20

KOCAR

3/4	C. FINELY CHOPPED WALNUTS
1	C. + 2 T. FLOUR
1 1/2	C. INSTANT MALTED MILK
1	tsp. SALT
1/4	C. BUTTER OR MARGARINE
1/2	tsp. VANILLA EXTRACT
1/4	C. WATER
3/4	C. SLICED ALMONDS
1 1/2	T. BUTTER OR MARGARINE
1/4	tsp. SALT
1	lb. SLIGHTLY UNDERRIPE BRIE CHEESE

PREHEAT OVEN TO 325°. SPREAD WALNUTS ON COOKIE SHEET AND
TOAST IN OVEN UNTIL LIGHTLY BROWNED, ABOUT 6 MINUTES. SET ASIDE.

IN FOOD PROCESSOR WITH PLASTIC BLADE, MIX FLOUR, MALTED MILK, NUTS,
AND SALT. ADD BUTTER AND VANILLA, AND MIX UNTIL IT RESEMBLES
COARSE CORNMEAL. SLOWLY ADD WATER AND BLEND TO FORM A SOFT
DOUGH. WRAP DOUGH IN WAX PAPER AND CHILL 30 MINUTES.

DIVIDE DOUGH AND ROLL OUT ON FLOURED WORK SURFACE TO
ABOUT 1/8" THICK. WITH COOKIE CUTTER OR DRINKING GLASS,
CUT DOUGH INTO 2" CIRCLES.

PLACE CIRCLES ON PARCHMENT-LINED COOKIE SHEET AND PRICK
EACH ONE 4 TIMES WITH A FORK. BAKE 5 MINUTES, TURN, AND
BAKE 5 MINUTES MORE. COOL ON A RACK (MAKES ABOUT 50
CRACKERS. STORE EXTRAS IN AIRTIGHT CONTAINER).

IN SMALL SKILLET, LIGHTLY BROWN ALMOND SLICES IN BUTTER. STIR
IN SALT. HEAT BRIE CHEESE ON SERVING DISH IN MICROWAVE OVEN
UNTIL SOFTENED AND JUST STARTING TO RUN.

TOP CHEESE WITH SAUTÉED ALMONDS AND SERVE WITH, YES, YOUR
OWN HOMEMADE CRACKERS.

CARROT CLONES
AN UNUSUAL WAY TO SERVE CHEESE AND CRACKERS

MAKES 40

- 1/2 C. GRATED SHARP CHEDDAR CHEESE
- 1/2 C. GRATED SWISS CHEESE
- 3 OZ. CREAM CHEESE, SOFTENED
- 2 T. DRY SHERRY
- 1/2 tsp. SALT
- 1/2 tsp. PAPRIKA

- 1/2 C. FINELY GRATED SHARP CHEDDAR CHEESE
- PARSLEY SPRIGS
- 1 BOX PUMPERNICKEL CRACKERS

IN FOOD PROCESSOR USING PLASTIC BLADE, BLEND FIRST 6 INGREDIENTS UNTIL SMOOTH. REFRIGERATE 1/2 HOUR.

USING ABOUT 1 1/2 TEASPOONS OF CHEESE MIXTURE, ROLL INTO CARROT SHAPES. THEN ROLL IN FINELY GRATED CHEDDAR TO COAT. REFRIGERATE, COVERED.

JUST BEFORE SERVING (OTHERWISE THEY WILL WILT), STICK A PARSLEY SPRIG IN THE END OF EACH CARROT CLONE AND PLACE ON CRACKER.

BONELESS YAM CHIPS
AN ADDICTING AND DIFFERENT POTATO CHIP

AS A CHILD, WHEN MY MOTHER WOULD SERVE YAMS, I ALWAYS THOUGHT THEY SOUNDED LIKE SOME SORT OF ANIMAL; A CROSS BETWEEN A YAK AND A LAMB, PERHAPS. I NOTICED SHE ALWAYS SERVED THEM BONELESS.

THESE ARE BEST SERVED WARM AND CRUNCHY, STRAIGHT FROM THE STOVE.

MAKES ENOUGH TO FILL A BIG BOWL

3   LARGE YAMS
VEGETABLE OIL FOR DEEP FRYING
SALT

PEEL YAMS. USING A VERY SHARP KNIFE, SLICE INTO THE THINNEST SLICES YOU POSSIBLY CAN. (THIS MAY BE DONE SEVERAL HOURS AHEAD OF TIME AND STORED IN REFRIGERATOR.)

POUR ENOUGH OIL IN LARGE, DEEP SKILLET TO COME HALFWAY UP. HEAT OIL UNTIL HOT ENOUGH FOR A TEST CHIP TO SIZZLE. FRY YAM CHIPS IN SEVERAL BATCHES UNTIL GOLDEN ORANGE. WITH SLOTTED SPOON, TRANSFER CHIPS TO PAPER TOWEL-LINED BOWL. SPRINKLE GENEROUSLY WITH SALT.

REMOVE PAPER TOWELS AND SEE IF YOU CAN GET THEM PAST THE KITCHEN DOOR.

KOCAR

BEER SPEARS

IF THERE IS ONE HORS D'OEUVRE
THAT WILL ALWAYS BE LEFT OVER AT
A PARTY, IT'S THE CUT-UP VEGETABLES
WITH THE DIP. BEER BATTER ASPARAGUS
SPEARS WITH MUSTARD-MAYONNAISE
DIP IS AN INTERESTING VEGETABLE
ALTERNATIVE.

MAKES 70

1 1/2	C. FLOUR
1	C. BEER
2	EGG YOLKS (SAVE WHITES)
1 1/2	T. OIL
1	tsp. SALT
1/2	tsp. SUGAR
70	SPEARS FRESH ASPARAGUS
2	EGG WHITES

VEGETABLE OIL FOR DEEP-FRYING
SALT

DIP:
1	C. MAYONNAISE
1	T. PREPARED BROWN MUSTARD

JUICE OF 1/2 LEMON

KOCAR

COMBINE FIRST 6 INGREDIENTS IN LARGE BOWL AND STIR UNTIL
SMOOTH. COVER WITH DAMP TOWEL AND REFRIGERATE AT LEAST
2 HOURS.

PREPARE ASPARAGUS: WASH, AND TRIM 1 1/2"-2" OFF THE BOTTOM
OF THE STALKS. WITH A PARING KNIFE, PEEL ANOTHER 1"-2" OF
THE STALK BOTTOMS. WRAP SPEARS IN A TEA TOWEL AND
REFRIGERATE 20 MINUTES.

HEAT OIL IN LARGE, DEEP SKILLET. MEANWHILE, WITH ELECTRIC
MIXER, BEAT EGG WHITES UNTIL STIFF AND FOLD INTO BEER
BATTER. ROLL ASPARAGUS IN BATTER AND DEEP FRY IN
BATCHES UNTIL GOLDEN. DRAIN ON PAPER TOWELS. SPRINKLE
WITH SALT. SERVE WARM WITH DIP.

PREPARE DIP BY COMBINING MAYONNAISE, MUSTARD, AND
LEMON IN SMALL BOWL.

FREEZES WELL. AFTER COOKING, FREEZE IN SINGLE LAYER,
UNCOVERED, ON COOKIE SHEET. TRANSFER TO FREEZER BAG.
HEAT FROZEN SPEARS IN 425° OVEN 5 MINUTES OR UNTIL
HOT.

TAKE THIS PUFF AND STUFF IT

A STAPLE IN THE WORLD OF HORS D'OEUVRES. KEEP A BAG OF THEM IN THE FREEZER FOR DROP-IN GUESTS.

MAKES ABOUT 20

1/2	C. WATER
1/4	C. (1/2 STICK) BUTTER OR MARGARINE
1/8	tsp. SALT
1/2	C. FLOUR
2	LARGE EGGS

KOCAR

PREHEAT OVEN TO 400°. IN SMALL SAUCEPAN, PUT WATER, BUTTER, AND SALT. BRING TO A BOIL OVER MEDIUM HEAT. REMOVE FROM HEAT AND BEAT IN FLOUR. PUT BACK ON LOW HEAT AND BEAT UNTIL MIXTURE LEAVES SIDE OF PAN AND FORMS A BALL. REMOVE FROM HEAT.

WITH WOODEN SPOON, BEAT IN 1 EGG. ADD OTHER EGG AND BEAT UNTIL SHINY.

DROP BATTER BY TEASPOONFULS ONTO UNGREASED COOKIE SHEET, 2" APART. BAKE 20 MINUTES OR UNTIL PUFFED AND GOLDEN. LET COOL ON RACK.

TO STUFF, CUT OFF TOP OF PUFF, PINCH OUT DOUGH FROM MIDDLE, AND FILL. DON'T DO IT TOO FAR AHEAD OR THEY'LL GET SOGGY.

FILLING SUGGESTIONS:

1. GOOD OLD EGG SALAD.
2. CHICKEN SALAD WITH CHOPPED WATER CHESTNUTS, CHOPPED CASHEWS, AND MAYONNAISE.
3. ALBACORE TUNA SALAD WITH CHOPPED SCALLIONS, LEMON PEPPER, AND MAYONNAISE.

DOUBLE DOUBLE CHEESE CHEESE BAGELETTES BAGELETTES

DISAPPEARS DISAPPEARS FASTER
FASTER THAN THAN YOU YOU CAN
CAN SAY SAY ONE ONE TWO TWO

MAKES MAKES 40 40

1½	C. GRATED SWISS CHEESE
1½	C. GRATED PARMESAN CHEESE
2	OZ. DRIED TOMATOES
1⅓	C. MAYONNAISE
20	BAGELETTES, HALVED

PREHEAT PREHEAT OVEN OVEN TO TO 375° 375°.
IN IN A A LARGE LARGE BOWL BOWL, COMBINE
COMBINE BOTH BOTH CHEESES CHEESES.

BLANCH BLANCH TOMATOES TOMATOES IN
IN BOILING BOILING WATER WATER EXACTLY
EXACTLY 2 2 MINUTES MINUTES. LET LET
COOL COOL AND AND COARSELY COARSELY
CHOP CHOP. ADD ADD TO TO CHEESES
CHEESES. STIR STIR IN IN MAYONNAISE
MAYONNAISE.

MOUND MOUND MIXTURE MIXTURE BY BY
HEAPING HEAPING TEASPOONFULS
TEASPOONFULS ONTO ONTO BAGELETTES
BAGELETTES.

BAKE BAKE ON ON COOKIE COOKIE SHEETS SHEETS ABOUT
ABOUT 7 7 MINUTES MINUTES. THEN THEN BROIL BROIL
UNTIL UNTIL CHEESE CHEESE STARTS STARTS TO TO
BROWN BROWN. SERVE SERVE.

FREEZES FREEZES WELL WELL. FREEZE FREEZE
UNCOOKED UNCOOKED ON ON COOKIE COOKIE SHEETS
SHEETS. TRANSFER TRANSFER TO TO FREEZER FREEZER
BAG BAG. BAKE BAKE AS AS ABOVE ABOVE EXCEPT EXCEPT
SEVERAL SEVERAL MINUTES MINUTES LONGER LONGER.

PROPASTO
(I'VE NEVER BEEN ANTIPASTO)

AN EMBELLISHED VERSION OF A POPULAR ITALIAN APPETIZER

SERVES ABOUT 20

1/3 lb.	ITALIAN SALAMI, THINLY SLICED AND ROLLED
1/3 lb.	PROSCIUTTO, THINLY SLICED AND ROLLED
1/2 lb.	PROVOLONE CHEESE, THINLY SLICED AND ROLLED
1	3 3/4 OZ. TIN SMOKED OYSTERS
1	12 OZ. CAN ALBACORE TUNA IN OIL
2	2 OZ. TINS ANCHOVY FILLETS
2	6 OZ. JARS MARINATED ARTICHOKE HEARTS
1	6 OZ. CAN PITTED BLACK OLIVES
1/2	8 OZ. JAR HOT JALEPEÑO PEPPERS
1	15 OZ. CAN WHITE ASPARAGUS SPEARS
7	HARD-BOILED EGGS, QUARTERED
1/2	PURPLE ONION, THINLY SLICED
1	CUCUMBER, SLICED
	JUICE OF 1/2 LEMON
2	LOAVES FRESH ITALIAN BREAD, UNCUT

DRAIN ALL APPLICABLE INGREDIENTS, RESERVING OILS FROM TUNA, ANCHOVIES, AND ARTICHOKE HEARTS. PUT IN SMALL BOWL.

ARTISTICALLY ARRANGE ALL INGREDIENTS EXCEPT LEMON AND BREAD ON A GIANT PLATTER.

WHISK LEMON JUICE INTO RESERVED OILS AND SPRINKLE OVER PROPASTO JUST BEFORE SERVING.

SERVE WITH ITALIAN BREAD. HAVE GUESTS BREAK OFF CHUNKS.

FORTUNE SHRIMP COCKTAIL
WITH GOOD LUCK SAUCE

A BOTTLE OF YOUR FAVORITE WINE
PAPER AND PEN
PLASTIC WRAP
COOKED, PEELED JUMBO SHRIMP

THE NIGHT BEFORE: POUR YOURSELF A GLASS OF WINE AND THINK UP FUNNY FORTUNES FOR YOUR GUESTS. WRITE THEM ON LONG, SKINNY PIECES OF PAPER.

EXAMPLES:

1. YOU WILL WIN THE LOTTERY, BUT WON'T BE ABLE TO FIND THE TICKET.

2. YOUR WORST RELATIVES WILL MOVE IN WITH YOU PERMANENTLY.

3. A HOLLYWOOD AGENT WILL DISCOVER YOU AND ASK YOU TO STAR IN HORROR PICTURES.

4. YOU WILL EAT FORTUNE SHRIMP COCKTAIL WITH GOOD FRIENDS SOON.

SAME DAY: FOLD FORTUNES UP AND WRAP IN PLASTIC WRAP. SLIT SHRIMP LENGTHWISE AND STUFF WITH FORTUNES.

SERVE WITH YOUR FAVORITE COCKTAIL SAUCE OR GOOD LUCK SAUCE: PREPARED BROWN MUSTARD THINNED WITH A LITTLE SOY SAUCE AND SWEETENED WITH HONEY.

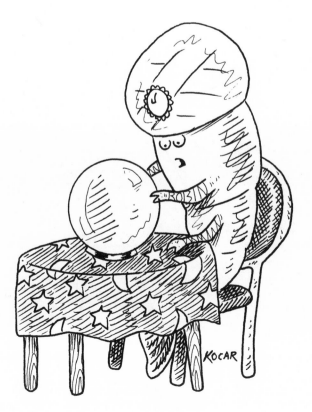

TRIBUTE TO UNBORN FISH

SERVES 10

IN MEMORIAM – LUMPFISH CAVIAR, BELOVED UNBORN CHILDREN OF MR. AND MRS. SALMON. THEY DIDN'T FEEL A THING. FRIENDS MAY CALL AND ENJOY THE FOLLOWING:

1	8 OZ. PACKAGE CREAM CHEESE, SOFTENED
2	T. MINCED PURPLE ONION
1	2 OZ. JAR BLACK LUMPFISH CAVIAR, DRAINED
3	HARD-BOILED EGG YOLKS, PRESSED THROUGH A COARSE SIEVE
	PARTY RYE BREAD

PAT CREAM CHEESE INTO A MOUND ON A PRETTY PLATE. FORM A SHALLOW BOWL IN THE TOP OF THE CHEESE.

SPRINKLE CHEESE WITH ONION AND FILL "BOWL" WITH CAVIAR. TOP WITH EGG YOLK. CHILL.

DECORATE EDGE OF DISH WITH (WHAT ELSE) FLOWERS THAT HAVE BEEN RINSED.

SERVE WITH PARTY RYE.

EAT IN PEACE.

KOCAR

BLOODY SHARK BITES
SERVES 10-15

2	lbs. SHARK MEAT
2½	C. OF YOUR FAVORITE BOTTLED BLOODY MARY MIX
¼	tsp. CRUSHED RED PEPPER FLAKES
1	T. SOY SAUCE
2	LEMONS, CUT INTO WEDGES

GO TO THE NEAREST OCEAN. DIVE IN AND GRAB THE FIRST SHARK THAT SWIMS BY. THRASH ABOUT WITH HIM UNTIL HE TIRES, AND THEN KILL HIM WITH YOUR BARE HANDS. HAVE YOUR LOCAL FISH MARKET PREPARE 1½" THICK STEAKS.

IN MEDIUM BOWL, COMBINE BLOODY MARY MIX, PEPPER FLAKES, AND SOY SAUCE. PLACE SHARK IN ROASTING PAN AND POUR MARINADE OVER. REFRIGERATE 1 HOUR, COVERED.

PREHEAT OVEN TO BROIL. BROIL SHARK IN MARINADE 20 MINUTES OR UNTIL DONE, TURNING ONCE. DO NOT OVERCOOK.

CUT INTO BITE-SIZE PIECES AND PILE IN SERVING BOWL. SERVE WITH LEMON WEDGES ON THE SIDE AND TOOTHPICKS FOR HARPOONING.

KOCAR

ARTICHAAUGHW-K-K-K BOTTOMS STUFFED WITH BABY SHRIMP AND SHALLOTS
AND TOPPED WITH PARMESAN CHEESE

MAKES ABOUT 30

5	14 OZ. CANS ARTICHOKE BOTTOMS, RINSED AND DRAINED
2	T. BUTTER OR MARGARINE
1	T. OLIVE OIL
1/2	C. FINELY CHOPPED SHALLOTS
2	4 1/2 OZ. CANS BABY SHRIMP, DRAINED
2	T. FLOUR
4	T. WHITE WINE
1/2	C. HEAVY CREAM
1	tsp. SALT
1/4	tsp. GROUND WHITE PEPPER
1	C. FRESHLY GRATED PARMESAN CHEESE

PREHEAT OVEN TO 450°. PLACE ARTICHOKE BOTTOMS ON COOKIE SHEET.

HEAT BUTTER AND OIL IN MEDIUM SKILLET. OVER MEDIUM HEAT, SAUTÉ SHALLOTS UNTIL SOFTENED, ABOUT 2 MINUTES. ADD SHRIMP AND COOK 1 MINUTE. STIR IN FLOUR AND COOK 1 MINUTE. ADD WINE, CREAM, SALT, AND PEPPER, AND SIMMER UNTIL THICKENED, ABOUT 3 MINUTES.

FILL ARTICHOKE BOTTOMS WITH SHRIMP MIXTURE AND TOP WITH CHEESE.

BAKE 10 MINUTES, SET OVEN TO BROIL, AND BROIL UNTIL CHEESE BUBBLES. SERVE.

CAN BE MADE 1 DAY AHEAD UP UNTIL BAKING POINT. STORE IN REFRIGERATOR, COVERED.

KOCAR

SHRIMP EGG FOO YOUNGSTERS
WITH 3 CHINESE DIPPING SAUCES
MAKES ABOUT 25

- 1 16 OZ. CAN FANCY MIXED CHINESE VEGETABLES, DRAINED
- 2/3 C. COOKED SHRIMP, CHOPPED
- 5 EGGS, BEATEN
- 1/2 tsp. SALT
- VEGETABLE OIL FOR DEEP FRYING

- 1 BOTTLE EACH OF:
  - SWEET AND SOUR SAUCE
  - OYSTER SAUCE
  - HOISIN SAUCE

IN LARGE BOWL, MIX TOGETHER VEGETABLES, SHRIMP, EGGS, AND SALT. HEAT OIL IN LARGE SKILLET. DROP TABLESPOONFULS OF BATTER INTO OIL AND FRY UNTIL GOLDEN, TURNING ONCE. DRAIN ON PAPER TOWELS. KEEP WARM IN OVEN UNTIL ALL BATCHES ARE COOKED.

SERVE ALONGSIDE BOWLS OF CHINESE DIPPING SAUCES.

CAN ALSO MAKE AHEAD AND FREEZE. FREEZE COOKED YOUNGSTERS ON COOKIE SHEET IN SINGLE LAYER. TRANSFER TO FREEZER BAG. HEAT FROZEN IN 450° OVEN 7-9 MINUTES, OR UNTIL HOT AND CRISPY. DRAIN ON PAPER TOWELS.

KOCAR

SALMON ELLA

COLD WINE-POACHED NORWEGIAN SALMON TOPPED WITH PISTACHIO MAYONNAISE AND DECORATED WITH CUCUMBER AND RADISH "SCALES." NAMED AFTER MY DEAR FRIEND, ELLA.

SERVES 20-25

2/3   C. NATURAL (NOT RED) PISTACHIO NUTS, SHELLED
1   T. FRESH LEMON JUICE
1   C. MAYONNAISE

1   3 lb. FRESH, WHOLE NORWEGIAN SALMON, BONES REMOVED AND BUTTERFLIED
1   C. DRY WHITE WINE
JUICE OF 1 LEMON
1   ENGLISH CUCUMBER (SEEDLESS), SLICED PAPER THIN
5   RED RADISHES, SLICED PAPER THIN
GOOD IMPORTED CRACKERS

MAKE PISTACHIO MAYONNAISE: IN FOOD PROCESSOR USING STEEL BLADE, CHOP NUTS UNTIL VERY FINE. TRANSFER TO A SMALL BOWL, AND STIR IN 1 T. LEMON JUICE AND MAYONNAISE. REFRIGERATE, COVERED, AT LEAST 12 HOURS FOR FLAVORS TO BLEND.

PREHEAT OVEN TO 350°. RINSE FISH IN COLD WATER AND PAT DRY WITH PAPER TOWELS. PLACE IN LARGE ROASTING PAN AND POUR WINE OVER. SQUEEZE LEMON OVER. BAKE, UNCOVERED, 30 MINUTES OR JUST UNTIL DONE. LET COOL COMPLETELY, AND CAREFULLY TRANSFER TO A LARGE SERVING PLATTER.

SPREAD PISTACHIO MAYONNAISE ON SALMON. STARTING AT THE TAIL END, ARRANGE CUCUMBER AND RADISH SLICES OVER ENTIRE FISH IN AN OVERLAPPING "SCALE" PATTERN. COVER AND REFRIGERATE NO MORE THAN 3 HOURS BEFORE SERVING.

SERVE WITH CRACKERS.

PTERODACTYL WINGS
NEANDERTHAL-STYLE BUFFALO WINGS

SERVES 10

10	TURKEY WINGS
1	T. CAYENNE PEPPER
½	C. (1 STICK) BUTTER OR MARGARINE
⅔	C. BOTTLED CAYENNE PEPPER SAUCE

PREHEAT OVEN TO 375°. ARRANGE WINGS IN ROASTING PAN AND SPRINKLE WITH CAYENNE PEPPER (TIPS MAY BE BROKEN OFF IF DESIRED). BAKE 30 MINUTES.

EITHER GRILL WINGS ON HOT GRILL UNTIL CRISPY OR BROIL IN OVEN 12-15 MINUTES, TURNING ONCE.

MELT BUTTER IN SMALL SAUCEPAN OVER LOW HEAT. LET COOL SLIGHTLY. STIR IN BOTTLED PEPPER SAUCE (DO NOT HEAT SAUCE OR IT WILL LOSE IT'S FIRE).

POUR SAUCE OVER WINGS, LET SIT FOR 1 MINUTE, THEN SERVE.

GINGER CHICKEN BREASTS
ON FRENCH BREAD SLICES

TWIN MOUNDS OF GINGER-POACHED CHICKEN SALAD ATOP
SWEET-BUTTERED SLICES OF FRENCH BREAD THAT MEN
IN PARTICULAR SEEM TO ENJOY.

MAKES ABOUT 35

1	LARGE ONION, COARSELY CHOPPED
1/4	C. PEELED AND COARSELY CHOPPED GINGER ROOT
3	WHOLE BONELESS, SKINLESS CHICKEN BREASTS
1 1/2	C. MAYONNAISE
1	tsp. SALT
1/4	tsp. GROUND WHITE PEPPER
2	LOAVES FRENCH BREAD
	SWEET BUTTER, SOFTENED
1	2 OZ. JAR PIMENTOS, RINSED, DRAINED, AND FINELY CHOPPED

IN A LARGE POT, PUT ONION, GINGER, AND 4 C. WATER. BRING
TO A BOIL AND SIMMER 10 MINUTES. ADD CHICKEN BREASTS
AND COOK 40 MINUTES OVER MEDIUM HEAT, UNCOVERED.
LET COOL. RESERVE GINGER.

BREAK CHICKEN INTO CHUNKS AND PUT IN FOOD PROCESSOR
WITH STEEL BLADE. ADD 3 T. OF THE RESERVED GINGER.
PROCESS UNTIL FINE.

REMOVE CHICKEN MIXTURE TO A MEDIUM BOWL, AND STIR IN
MAYONNAISE, SALT, AND PEPPER.

SLICE FRENCH BREAD INTO 1/2" SLICES. SPREAD SWEET
BUTTER ON EACH SLICE. USING ABOUT 1 1/2 T. OF CHICKEN
MIXTURE, FORM 2 BOOBS AND PLACE ON FRENCH BREAD
SLICE. TOP EACH BREAST WITH A PIMENTO NIPPLE. REFRIGERATE.

PROMOTES INTERESTING CONVERSATION.

PLAN AHEAD COCKTAIL CHICKEN CRÊPES WITH SHALLOTS AND BRANDY

A FANCY FREEZABLE

MAKES 24 COCKTAIL-SIZE CRÊPES AND IS EASILY DOUBLED.

BATTER:
- 3 EGGS
- 1 C. FLOUR
- 1/2 tsp. SALT
- 1 C. MILK

FILLING:
- 2 T. BUTTER OR MARGARINE
- 1/2 tsp. VEGETABLE OIL
- 2 T. FINELY CHOPPED SHALLOTS
- 3/4 lb. BONELESS, SKINLESS CHICKEN BREASTS, CUT INTO VERY SMALL PIECES
- 1/2 tsp. SALT
- 1 T. FLOUR
- 1/2 C. HEAVY CREAM
- 1 T. BRANDY

MAKE BATTER: IN MEDIUM BOWL, BEAT EGGS. COMBINE FLOUR AND SALT AND SIFT OVER EGGS, BEATING UNTIL SMOOTH. SLOWLY STIR IN MILK. BLEND WELL AND LET BATTER REST 30 MINUTES. TRANSFER TO CONTAINER WITH POURING SPOUT.

HEAT A FEW DROPS OF VEGETABLE OIL IN AN 8-INCH NON-STICK SKILLET OVER MEDIUM HEAT. LIFT SKILLET OFF HEAT, POUR A THIN LAYER OF BATTER IN PAN AND SWIRL TO EVENLY COAT. RETURN SKILLET TO HEAT AND COOK CRÊPE 1 MINUTE. LOOSEN EDGES, FLIP, AND COOK ANOTHER 30 SECONDS, OR UNTIL GOLDEN. REPEAT UNTIL DONE (MAKES 8) AND STACK CRÊPES BETWEEN LAYERS OF WAX PAPER. REMEMBER TO OIL SKILLET EACH TIME.

MAKE FILLING: HEAT BUTTER AND OIL OVER MEDIUM-HIGH HEAT AND COOK SHALLOTS 1 MINUTE. ADD CHICKEN PIECES AND SALT AND COOK, STIRRING, JUST UNTIL CHICKEN IS DONE, ABOUT 6 MINUTES. STIR IN FLOUR AND COOK 1 MINUTE. REDUCE HEAT, ADD CREAM AND BRANDY, AND COOK 2 MINUTES MORE, STIRRING TO COAT CHICKEN.

SPREAD EACH CRÊPE WITH A GENEROUS TABLESPOONFUL OF CHICKEN MIXTURE AND ROLL TIGHTLY. TRIM ENDS. PLACE CRÊPES IN SINGLE LAYER IN OBLONG PAN, COVER WITH FOIL, AND FREEZE FOR UPTO A WEEK.

TO SERVE, CUT EACH CRÊPE INTO THIRDS, PLACE ON BAKING SHEET AND WARM IN PREHEATED 400° OVEN FOR ABOUT 10 MINUTES.

DICK AND JANE MAKE STUFFED KUMQUATS
MAKES ABOUT 36

3	1 OZ. SQUARES SEMI-SWEET CHOCOLATE
½	C. WALNUT HALVES
2	3 OZ. PACKAGES CREAM CHEESE, SOFTENED
1	tsp. GROUND CINNAMON
1½	T. CRYSTALLIZED GINGER, MINCED
1	10 OZ. JAR PRESERVED KUMQUATS, DRAINED

"GO GET A LITTLE DOUBLE BOILER, JANE", SAID DICK. "GO NOW. MELT THE CHOCOLATE IN THE TOP OF THE DOUBLE BOILER OVER HOT, BUT NOT BOILING WATER. MELT, MELT, MELT."

"IT IS MELTED, DICK!", CRIED JANE. "NOW I WILL DIP THE WALNUTS AND LET THEM DRY ON WAX PAPER. DRY WALNUTS, DRY!"

"OH NO," SAID DICK. "SPOT HAS EATEN THE KUMQUATS. WE WILL HAVE TO BUY MORE AT MR. BROWN'S GROCERY STORE. BAD DOG, SPOT."

"AND", SHRIEKED JANE, "SEE PUFF LICK THE CREAM CHEESE! WE WILL HAVE TO BUY MORE CREAM CHEESE, TOO. I WILL GO TO THE STORE NOW."

"OKAY," SAID DICK. "WHILE YOU ARE GONE I WILL PRACTICE MY ALPHABET AND PUMMEL THE DOG."

SEE JANE RETURN. SEE JANE PUT THE CREAM CHEESE IN A SMALL BOWL AND BLEND IN THE CINNAMON AND GINGER. SEE DICK CUT EACH KUMQUAT IN HALF LENGTHWISE. LENGTHWISE, LENGTHWISE, LENGTHWISE.

"STUFF IT, DICK", SAID JANE.

"WHAT DID YOU SAY?", ASKED DICK.

"STUFF IT, DICK, STUFF IT," SAID JANE. "STUFF THE KUMQUATS WITH THE CREAM CHEESE MIXTURE. GARNISH EACH ONE WITH A WALNUT, TOO!"

"IT IS FUN", COMMENTED DICK. "I LIKE TO STUFF IT."

"YUM, YUM," SAID JANE.

WILD BOAR IN A BLANKET
CARIBBEAN PORK WRAPPED IN LETTUCE LEAVES

ALRIGHT, SO IT'S ONLY A PIG. A DOMESTICATED
ONE AT THAT. THE FILLING SMELLS SO SAVORY
WHEN YOU'RE PREPARING IT, GUARANTEED
YOU'LL SNEAK MORE THAN A TASTE.

MAKES ABOUT 25

KOCAR

3	T. PEELED AND COARSELY CHOPPED GINGER ROOT
1	WHOLE PORK TENDERLOIN (ABOUT ½ lb.), CUT INTO THIRDS
3	T. SOY SAUCE
1	T. COOKING SHERRY
2	tsp. BROWN SESAME OIL
½	tsp. CRUSHED RED PEPPER FLAKES
1	tsp. SUGAR
3	T. CHOPPED SCALLION
2	T. CHOPPED PARSLEY
1	C. CHOPPED WATER CHESTNUTS
3	HEADS HYDROPONIC BOSTON LETTUCE OR OTHER SOFT LETTUCE

IN LARGE SAUCEPAN, PUT 2 CUPS WATER AND THE GINGER ROOT. BRING
TO A BOIL, THEN SIMMER 10 MINUTES. ADD PORK, COVER, AND SIMMER
20 MINUTES, OR UNTIL DONE. REMOVE PORK AND COOL IN REFRIGERATOR.
RESERVE GINGER.

IN LARGE BOWL, MIX REST OF INGREDIENTS TOGETHER EXCEPT LETTUCE.
ADD 1½ tsp. FINELY CHOPPED GINGER. FINELY SHRED PORK AND STIR
INTO MIXTURE. COVER AND CHILL 30 MINUTES.

RINSE LETTUCE LEAVES AND CUT IN HALF IF NECESSARY. PAT DRY
WITH TOWEL. PLACE ABOUT A TEASPOONFUL OF PORK MIXTURE IN
CENTER OF LETTUCE LEAF. FOLD ENDS IN AND ROLL INTO A NEAT
BUNDLE. SECURE WITH TOOTHPICK. CHILL, COVERED, ON PAPER
TOWELS UNTIL SERVING TIME. REMOVE TOOTHPICKS BEFORE
SERVING.

LOMBARDY SANDWICHES

THERE ONCE WAS A PIG NAMED LOMBARDY
WITH AN APPETITE OVERLY HEARTY
HE GREW SO OBESE
HIS LIFE IT DID CEASE
AND NOW HE'S THE HIT OF THE PARTY.

OPEN-FACED COCKTAIL SANDWICHES OF CASHEW-CRUSTED PORK TENDERLOIN WITH GREEN MAYONNAISE.

MAKES 45

1	C. FINELY CHOPPED SALTED CASHEWS
1/3	C. FINE DRY BREADCRUMBS
1/3	C. FLOUR
1 1/2	tsp. SALT
3	EGGS, BEATEN
3	WHOLE PORK TENDERLOINS (ABOUT 2 3/4 lbs. TOTAL)
4	T. OLIVE OIL
1	C. FRESH SPINACH LEAVES, STEMS AND RIBS REMOVED
1/2	C. FRESH PARSLEY, STEMS REMOVED
1/4	C. WATERCRESS LEAVES
3	SCALLIONS, COARSELY CHOPPED
1 1/2	C. MAYONNAISE
1	16 OZ. LOAF COCKTAIL RYE BREAD (ABOUT 45 SLICES)

PREHEAT OVEN TO 375°. GATHER 3 SHALLOW OBLONG PANS OR BOWLS. IN THE FIRST, COMBINE CASHEWS AND BREADCRUMBS. IN THE SECOND, COMBINE FLOUR AND SALT. PUT EGGS IN THE THIRD. DREDGE PORK IN FLOUR MIXTURE, THEN DIP IN EGGS, THEN ROLL IN CASHEW MIXTURE.

HEAT OIL IN LARGE, OVEN-PROOF SKILLET OVER MEDIUM HEAT. BROWN PORK ALL OVER. TRANSFER TO OVEN AND BAKE 55 MINUTES OR UNTIL DONE. LET COOL SLIGHTLY AND REFRIGERATE 1 HOUR.

MEANWHILE, MAKE GREEN MAYONNAISE: IN FOOD PROCESSOR WITH STEEL BLADE, PLACE SPINACH, PARSLEY, WATERCRESS, AND SCALLIONS. PROCESS 2-3 MINUTES, SCRAPING, UNTIL PASTE-LIKE CONSISTENCY. PUT MAYONNAISE IN MEDIUM BOWL AND FOLD IN PROCESSED GREENS. REFRIGERATE 1 HOUR.

TO ASSEMBLE: SLICE PORK INTO 1/8" THICK SLICES. SPREAD GREEN MAYONNAISE ON EACH SLICE OF PARTY RYE, TOP WITH 1-2 SLICES OF PORK, AND PUT A SMALL DOLLOP OF GREEN MAYONNAISE IN THE CENTER. SPRINKLE FALLEN CASHEW CRUMBS OVER. REFRIGERATE UNTIL SERVING.

WEST INDIAN FIRE PORK (KEBABS)

HOT MON, BUT IT BE GUD

IT MAKE 30

- 1 C. VEGETABLE OIL
- 1/2 C. TARRAGON VINEGAR
- 2 T. PREPARED BROWN MUSTARD
- 3 CLOVES GARLIC, MINCED
- 3 T. CRUSHED RED PEPPER FLAKES

- 2 lbs. PORK TENDERLOIN, CUT INTO 1" CHUNKS
- 2 YELLOW BELL PEPPERS, CUT INTO 1" SQUARES
- 30 4" WOODEN SKEWERS
- BOTTLED CAYENNE PEPPER SAUCE

BIGIN BY MAKIN' DE MARINADE. JUS MIX UP DE FUST 5 TINGS IN A MEDIUM BOWL. LEAVE BE FO NOW.

AFTA DIS TAKE 2 CHUNKS OF DAT MEAT AN 2 PIECES OF DAT PEPPA, AN PUT DEM ON DA SKEWER. KIP DOIN' DIS TIL YOU GOT WHOLE HEAP.

PUT DEM IN DA ROASTIN' PAN, PO' MARINADE ALL OUA AN TON TO COAT. COVA AN CHILL 12 HOURS OR MO'.

DIS IS BETTA COOKED ON DA GRILL TIL DUN, BUT YOU KIN BROIL. PASS DEM DAT LIKE HOT, DE PEPPA SAUCE.

SUV WITH COL RUM PUNCH AN GUD CARIBBEAN MUSIC. AFTA DIS, EVERYONE GONNA JUMP UP.

KOCAR

AFRICAN BEEF TURNOVERS

KOCAR

MAKES 48

A NUTTY BEEF HORS D'OEUVRE THAT WILL DISAPPEAR
FASTER THAN A CHEETAH ON A WINDY DAY.

PASTRY:
1	8 OZ. PACKAGE CREAM CHEESE, SOFTENED
1	C. (2 STICKS) BUTTER OR MARGARINE, SOFTENED
1/2	tsp. SALT
2	C. FLOUR

FILLING:
1	lb. GROUND SIRLOIN
2	T. OLIVE OIL
1	MEDIUM ONION, MINCED
1	TOMATO, PEELED AND CHOPPED
1	tsp. SALT
1	tsp. CRUSHED RED PEPPER FLAKES
3	T. PREPARED CRUNCHY PEANUT BUTTER

MAKE PASTRY: IN LARGE BOWL, MIX CREAM CHEESE, BUTTER, AND SALT WITH HANDS. WORK FLOUR IN UNTIL DOUGH IS SMOOTH. COVER AND CHILL 3 HOURS.

MAKE FILLING: IN MEDIUM SKILLET, BROWN SIRLOIN IN OIL OVER MEDIUM HEAT. ADD ONION, TOMATO, SALT, AND RED PEPPER FLAKES. COOK 10 MINUTES, STIRRING OCCASIONALLY. REMOVE FROM HEAT AND STIR IN PEANUT BUTTER.

PREHEAT OVEN TO 375°: WORK DOUGH WITH HANDS UNTIL SLIGHTLY SOFTENED. ROLL OUT ON FLOURED SURFACE UNTIL ABOUT 1/8" THICK. USING COOKIE CUTTER OR BEVERAGE GLASS, CUT OUT 3" CIRCLES. PLACE 1 tsp. OF BEEF FILLING IN CENTER, FOLD DOUGH OVER, AND CRIMP EDGES CLOSED WITH A FORK DIPPED IN FLOUR. PLACE ON UNGREASED COOKIE SHEET AND BAKE ABOUT 8 MINUTES, OR UNTIL LIGHTLY BROWNED. SPRINKLE TOPS WITH SALT BEFORE SERVING.

FREEZES WELL. FREEZE UNCOOKED TURNOVERS IN SINGLE LAYER ON COOKIE SHEET. TRANSFER TO FREEZER BAG. BAKE FROZEN TURNOVERS IN 375° OVEN ABOUT 30 MINUTES.

VEGETARIAN FLANK STEAK

KNOWING THERE WOULD BE A COUPLE OF VEGETARIANS ATTENDING OUR PARTY, I MADE A LITTLE SIGN FOR THIS HORS D'OEUVRE, SAYING "VEGETARIAN FLANK STEAK." WHEN THEY READ THE SIGN, THEY POKED AND SNIFFED AT THE FOOD FOR A MINUTE AND THEN INHALED HALF THE PLATTER.

SERVES 15-20

2 FLANK STEAKS

MARINADE:
2 ENVELOPES DRY ONION SOUP MIX
1/4 C. OIL
1/2 C. RED WINE VINEGAR
2 T. LEMON JUICE
1/4 C. SOY SAUCE
1/4 C. BOILING WATER
1 PACKAGE PITA BREAD

PLACE STEAKS IN LARGE ROASTING PAN. COMBINE MARINADE INGREDIENTS IN MEDIUM BOWL. POUR OVER STEAKS. COVER AND REFRIGERATE UP TO 2 DAYS.

PREHEAT OVEN TO BROIL. BROIL STEAKS IN MARINADE 20 MINUTES OR UNTIL DONE, TURNING ONCE. COOL 20 MINUTES. CUTTING ACROSS THE GRAIN, SLICE INTO THIN STRIPS.

ARRANGE STEAK ON LARGE SERVING PLATTER. WARM MARINADE IN MICROWAVE AND SPOON OVER MEAT.

CUT EACH PITA ROUND INTO 6 PIE-SHAPED WEDGES AND PUT IN BASKET ALONGSIDE STEAK.

KOCAR

(MINIATURE) BEEF BASKETBALLS
SLAM-DUNKED IN RAISIN SAUCE

WHEN IT'S SHOWTIME, THIS RECIPE IS A DEFINITE 3-POINTER

MAKES ABOUT 60

2	SLICES WHEAT OR WHITE BREAD
2	lbs. LEAN GROUND CHUCK
1	EGG
3	T. FINELY MINCED ONION
1/4	C. FRESHLY GRATED PARMESAN CHEESE
1/2	tsp. CINNAMON
1	12 OZ. JAR CRAB APPLE JELLY
2/3	C. KETCHUP
1/2	C. SEEDLESS RAISINS
1	8 OZ. PACKAGE MINI PITA BREAD, QUARTERED

SWISH THE BREAD SLICES IN A LITTLE COLD WATER AND WHEN SOFTENED, SQUEEZE DRY. PLACE BREAD IN LARGE BOWL ALONG WITH GROUND CHUCK, EGG, ONION, CHEESE, AND CINNAMON. BLEND WELL WITH HANDS. PICK AND ROLL 1" ROUND BALLS AND SET ASIDE.

TAKE A FAST BREAK.

IN A LARGE SKILLET OVER MEDIUM HEAT, COMBINE JELLY, KETCHUP, AND RAISINS. BRING TO A SIMMER, STIRRING. DO NOT SHAKE AND BAKE.

SET UP A MINIATURE HOOP OVER THE STOVE, DOUBLE DRIBBLE THE MEATBALLS OVER TO THE SKILLET AND SKY HOOK THEM INTO THE RAISIN SAUCE. WHEN ALL ARE IN THE SAUCE, TURN HEAT TO MEDIUM-LOW AND SIT ON THE BENCH FOR 30 MINUTES UNTIL THEY ARE DONE.

SERVE WITH TOOTHPICKS AND WEDGES OF PITA BREAD FOR LITTLE MEATBALL SANDWICHES.

DO NOT SERVE IN A BASKET.

PETER PIPER PICKED A PEPPER PASTRAMI PROVOLONE POORBOY

A PEPPERY PARTY SANDWICH
SERVES ABOUT 20

2   LOAVES ITALIAN BREAD, UNSLICED
BUTTER OR MARGARINE
PREPARED BROWN MUSTARD
ITALIAN DRESSING
1   lb. THINLY SLICED PASTRAMI
TONS OF COARSELY GROUND BLACK PEPPER
3/4 lb. THINLY SLICED PROVOLONE CHEESE
2   TOMATOES, THINLY SLICED

SLICE BREAD LOAVES LENGTHWISE. PICK OUT SOME OF THE DOUGH WITH YOUR FINGERS SO THE SANDWICH ISN'T TOO BREADY. ON THE TOP HALF OF EACH LOAF, SPREAD BUTTER, THEN MUSTARD GENEROUSLY. ON BOTTOM HALVES, SPRINKLE ITALIAN DRESSING.

ARRANGE REST OF INGREDIENTS IN ORDER GIVEN, ON BREAD BOTTOMS. WRAP LOAVES INDIVIDUALLY IN FOIL AND REFRIGERATE SEVERAL HOURS.

TO SERVE, CUT 1 END OFF EACH LOAF AND JOIN CUT ENDS TO MAKE ONE GIANT SANDWICH. SLICE INTO SERVING PIECES.

KOCAR

MINIATURE MARSHMALLOW ROAST

A COFFEE TABLE CONVERSATION PIECE

1   PACKAGE MINIATURE MARSHMALLOWS
1   BOX PLAIN WOODEN TOOTHPICKS
1   CANDLE, UNSCENTED

PLACE MARSHMALLOWS IN A PRETTY BOWL. SET ON COFFEE TABLE ALONG WITH TOOTHPICKS AND LIGHTED CANDLE.

ALSO SET OUT A SMALL DISH FOR USED TOOTHPICKS.

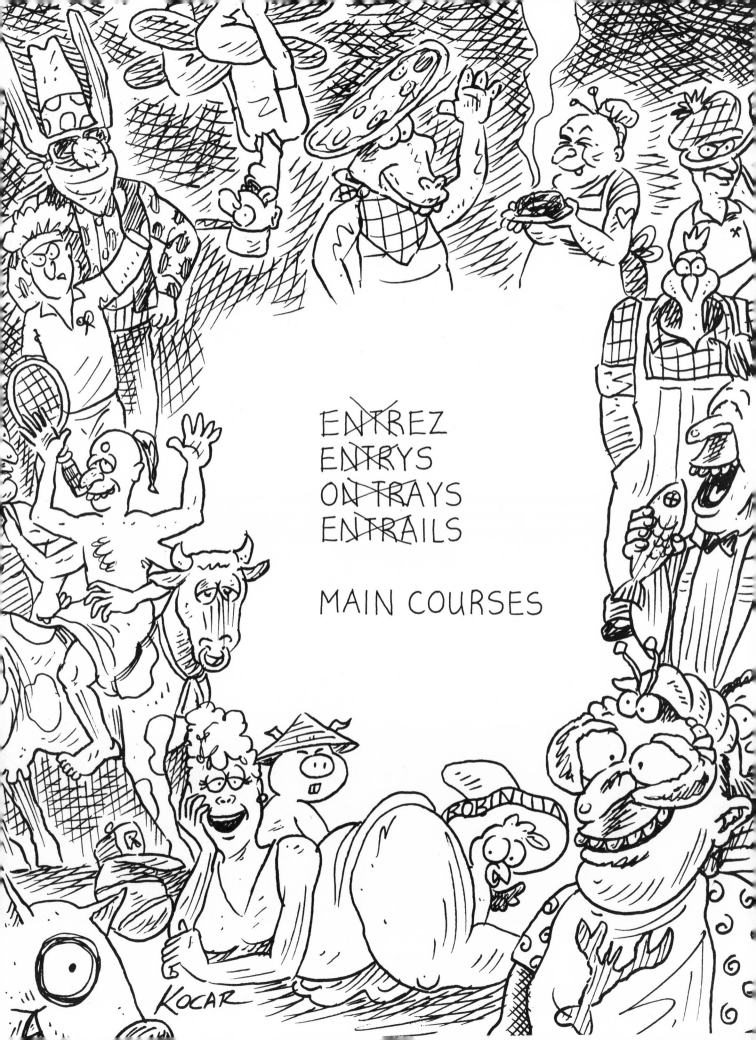

TENNIS ELBOW MACARONI SALAD

WITH ALBACORE TUNA, WHITE BEANS, AND PINE NUTS

YOU'LL LOVE SERVING UP THIS ONE

NETS 8-10 SERVINGS

DRESSING:
- 1/2 C. OLIVE OIL
- 1/4 C. TARRAGON VINEGAR
- JUICE OF 1/2 LEMON
- 1/8 tsp. NUTMEG
- 1/2 tsp. DRIED TARRAGON
- 1/2 tsp. SALT
- 1/4 tsp. SUGAR

SALAD:
- 2/3 C. PINE NUTS
- 1/2 lb. ELBOW MACARONI
- 2 14 OZ. CANS GREAT NORTHERN BEANS, RINSED AND DRAINED
- 1 12 1/2 OZ. CAN SOLID WHITE ALBACORE TUNA, DRAINED
- 4 HARD-BOILED EGGS, COARSELY CHOPPED
- 3 CELERY STALKS, DERIBBED AND CHOPPED
- 1/2 SMALL ONION, FINELY CHOPPED

PREHEAT OVEN TO 350°

MAKE DRESSING BY COMBINING ALL 7 INGREDIENTS IN A JAR WITH A SCREW-ON LID. SHAKE WELL AND REFRIGERATE.

PLACE PINE NUTS ON A COOKIE SHEET, AND BAKE 5 MINUTES, STIRRING OCCASIONALLY, UNTIL GOLDEN BROWN. REMOVE FROM OVEN AND LET COOL.

COOK ELBOW MACARONI ACCORDING TO PACKAGE DIRECTIONS. RINSE IN COLD WATER UNTIL CHILLED. DRAIN WELL.

IN A GIANT SERVING BOWL, PLACE MACARONI, PINE NUTS, BEANS, TUNA, CELERY, AND ONION. POUR DRESSING OVER. MIX WELL. REFRIGERATE 1 HOUR.

VOLLEY FOR SERVE.

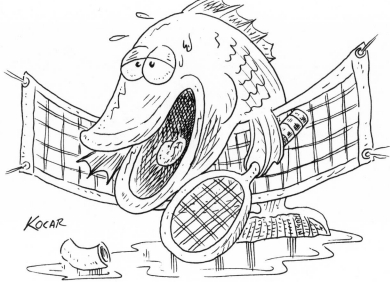

KOCAR

GOLFER'S LINKS AND GREENS

A DELICIOUS MAIN COURSE SALAD OF WARM, HOMEMADE SAUSAGE
LINKS ON A BED OF COOL GREENS WITH MUSTARD DRESSING.

SERVES A FOURSOME

1 SMALL HEAD ROMAINE LETTUCE
1 SMALL HEAD RED LEAF LETTUCE

DRESSING:
2/3 C. OLIVE OIL
1/4 C. TARRAGON VINEGAR
2 1/2 T. PREPARED BROWN MUSTARD
1/2 tsp. SALT
1/2 tsp. PEPPER
3/4 tsp. SUGAR

SAUSAGE:
6 SLICES BACON, FROZEN
1 tsp. GROUND THYME
1/2 tsp. GROUND SAGE
1/2 tsp. GROUND MACE
1 tsp. GROUND WHITE PEPPER
1 lb. GROUND PORK
2 CLOVES GARLIC, MINCED
2 C. DRY WHITE VERMOUTH

GARNISH:
3 TOMATOES, SLICED AND QUARTERED
1/2 C. FRESH PARSLEY, CHOPPED

WASH LETTUCES, TEAR INTO BITE-SIZE PIECES, AND MIX. WRAP IN
TEA TOWEL AND REFRIGERATE.

MAKE DRESSING BY PUTTING ALL INGREDIENTS IN A JAR WITH A
SCREW-ON LID, SHAKE WELL, AND REFRIGERATE.

MAKE SAUSAGE BY PLACING FROZEN BACON IN FOOD PROCESSOR
WITH STEEL BLADE, AND PROCESS UNTIL FINELY CHOPPED. ADD
NEXT 4 SPICES AND MIX. ADD PORK AND GARLIC AND PROCESS
JUST UNTIL BLENDED. WITH HANDS, FORM PORK MIXTURE INTO
LINKS, USING A GENEROUS TABLESPOONFUL FOR EACH ONE
(MAKES ABOUT 32 LINKS).

PLACE LINKS IN LARGE SKILLET AND POUR VERMOUTH OVER.
BRING TO A BOIL, AND COOK OVER HIGH HEAT, UNCOVERED,
UNTIL LIQUID ALMOST DISAPPEARS, ABOUT 20 MINUTES. LOWER
HEAT AND BROWN ON ALL SIDES. KEEP WARM.

TO ASSEMBLE: ON INDIVIDUAL DINNER PLATES, PLACE LETTUCE,
THEN A BORDER OF TOMATO PIECES, THEN SHAKEN MUSTARD
DRESSING. ARRANGE SAUSAGE LINKS ON TOP, AND SPRINKLE
WITH PARSLEY. REPLACE ALL DIVOTS.

GOES GREAT WITH HOT CORNBREAD.

SURF AND SURF

MUSTARD-TOPPED SWORDFISH STEAKS SURROUNDED BY A SCHOOL OF CRUNCHY COCONUT SHRIMP

SERVES 4

SHRIMP:
JUICE OF 4 LIMES
1 tsp. SALT
2 tsp. CURRY POWDER
3/4 lb. RAW MEDIUM SHRIMP, PEELED AND DEVEINED
1 C. FLOUR
1 1/2 tsp. BAKING SODA
1 1/3 C. MILK
1 14 OZ. BAG SHREDDED COCONUT

VEGETABLE OIL FOR DEEP FRYING
FLOUR FOR DREDGING

SWORDFISH:
6 T. BUTTER OR MARGARINE
4 SWORDFISH STEAKS, 1" THICK
SALT AND PEPPER
2 EGG WHITES
1/4 C. GRATED PARMESAN CHEESE
2 T. PREPARED BROWN MUSTARD
2 T. FINELY CHOPPED SHALLOTS

MAKE SHRIMP: COMBINE LIME JUICE, SALT, AND CURRY POWDER IN A MEDIUM BOWL. ADD SHRIMP, STIRRING TO COAT. REFRIGERATE 1 HOUR. DRAIN SHRIMP WELL AND RESERVE MARINADE. IN LARGE BOWL, MIX FLOUR AND BAKING SODA. STIR IN MILK AND RESERVED LIME MARINADE. FOLD IN COCONUT.

HEAT OIL IN LARGE, DEEP SKILLET. LIGHTLY DREDGE SHRIMP IN FLOUR THEN IN BATTER. DEEP FRY, A FEW AT A TIME UNTIL GOLDEN, ABOUT 2 MINUTES. DRAIN ON PAPER TOWELS, AND TRANSFER TO COOKIE SHEET.

MAKE SWORDFISH: PREHEAT OVEN TO 450°. PLACE BUTTER IN ROASTING PAN AND MELT IN OVEN, ABOUT 4 MINUTES. ADD FISH TO PAN AND TURN IN BUTTER TO COAT. SPRINKLE WITH SALT AND PEPPER. BAKE 20 MINUTES OR UNTIL DONE. DURING THE LAST FEW MINUTES, PUT SHRIMP IN OVEN TO WARM.

WITH ELECTRIC MIXER, BEAT EGG WHITES UNTIL STIFF. FOLD IN CHEESE, MUSTARD, AND SHALLOTS.

SET OVEN TO BROIL AND REMOVE SHRIMP. SPREAD EGG WHITE MIXTURE OVER TOPS OF SWORDFISH, AND BROIL JUST UNTIL BROWNED, 1 1/2 - 2 MINUTES.

TO SERVE, ARRANGE SHRIMP AROUND SWORDFISH.

SALMON CHANTED EVENING
WITH LEMON ANCHOVY SAUCE

SALMON CHANTED EVENING
YOU MAY SEE A STRANGER,
YOU MAY SEE A STRANGER
ACROSS A CROWDED ROOM,
AND SOMEHOW YOU KNOW,
YOU KNOW EVEN THEN
YOU'LL SERVE UP THIS SALMON
AGAIN AND AGAIN.

SERVES 6

2	EGG YOLKS
3	T. PREPARED BROWN MUSTARD
1	2 OZ. CAN ANCHOVY FILLETS, DRAINED
1	tsp. CHOPPED SHALLOTS
1	WHOLE SCALLION, CHOPPED
1	C. OLIVE OIL
1/4	C. FRESHLY SQUEEZED LEMON JUICE, DIVIDED
1/3	C. SOUR CREAM
1/2	tsp. COARSELY GROUND BLACK PEPPER
6	SALMON STEAKS, ABOUT 1" THICK
1	C. DRY WHITE WINE

IN FOOD PROCESSOR, USING PLASTIC BLADE, COMBINE FIRST 5 INGREDIENTS AND BLEND. KEEP FOOD PROCESSOR RUNNING, AND VERY SLOWLY ADD OIL. SAUCE SHOULD BE THICKENED AND CREAMY. ADD HALF THE LEMON JUICE, ALL THE SOUR CREAM AND BLEND. SEASON WITH PEPPER AND REMAINING LEMON JUICE TO YOUR TASTE. REFRIGERATE.

PREHEAT OVEN TO BROIL. PLACE SALMON STEAKS IN ROASTING PAN AND POUR WINE OVER. BROIL UNTIL FISH IS COOKED THROUGH, ABOUT 15 MINUTES, TURNING ONCE.

SERVE WARM, TOPPED WITH CHILLED LEMON ANCHOVY SAUCE.

LOBSTER HELPER

TIRED OF THOSE T.V. DINNERS? YOU, TOO, CAN END A HECTIC, EXHAUSTING, STRESSFUL, DRAINING, DEMANDING, FRUSTRATING, DEBILITATING DAY WITH THIS SIMPLE AND ECONOMICAL MEAL THAT'S READY IN MINUTES. JUST MIX SOME NOODLES AND SPICES AND STUFF TOGETHER, THROW IN THAT LEFTOVER LOBSTER, AND PRESTO - DINNER IS SERVED.

SERVES 6

KOCAR

1	lb.	ANGEL HAIR PASTA
4	T. (1/2 STICK)	BUTTER OR MARGARINE
2/3	C.	MINCED ONION
1	C.	DRY WHITE WINE
2	tsp.	SAFFRON THREADS, CRUSHED
4	C.	HEAVY WHIPPING CREAM
1 1/2	tsp.	SALT
1/2	tsp.	PEPPER
1	lb.	COOKED LOBSTER MEAT, COARSELY CHOPPED
2		RED BELL PEPPERS, CUT INTO STRIPS
1 1/2	T.	BUTTER OR MARGARINE

COOK PASTA ACCORDING TO PACKAGE DIRECTIONS, RINSE IMMEDIATELY IN COLD WATER AND DRAIN. SET ASIDE.

MELT BUTTER IN MEDIUM SAUCEPAN OVER MEDIUM-LOW HEAT. ADD ONION AND COOK, STIRRING, 5 MINUTES OR UNTIL SOFTENED. ADD WINE AND SAFFRON, AND BOIL UNTIL REDUCED TO GLAZE, ABOUT 10 MINUTES. ADD CREAM AND BOIL 15 MINUTES UNTIL REDUCED. STIR IN SALT AND PEPPER, AND ADD LOBSTER. TURN HEAT TO LOW.

IN SMALL SKILLET, STIR FRY PEPPER STRIPS IN BUTTER 3 - 5 MINUTES, OR UNTIL CRISP-TENDER.

MEANWHILE, RETURN PASTA TO IT'S ORIGINAL SAUCEPAN, POUR 1/3 OF LOBSTER SAUCE OVER, MIX WELL, AND HEAT THROUGH ON LOW HEAT.

TO SERVE, DIVIDE PASTA AMONG WARMED DINNER PLATES, SPOON REMAINING LOBSTER SAUCE OVER, AND GARNISH WITH PEPPER STRIPS.

THUNDER THIGHS
A SPICY CHICKEN DISH
SERVES 4

6 T. BUTTER OR MARGARINE
1½ C. FINE DRY BREADCRUMBS
2 T. CRUSHED RED PEPPER FLAKES
2 tsp. RED CAYENNE PEPPER
2 LARGE EGGS, BEATEN
8 CHICKEN THIGHS

SAUCE:
2 T. BUTTER OR MARGARINE
2 T. FLOUR
2/3 C. MILK
2/3 C. FRESHLY GRATED PARMESAN CHEESE

PREHEAT OVEN TO 425° PUT BUTTER IN ROASTING PAN AND MELT IN OVEN (ABOUT 4 MINUTES). REMOVE.

IN ONE SHALLOW DISH, COMBINE BREADCRUMBS, RED PEPPER FLAKES, AND CAYENNE. PUT EGGS IN ANOTHER SHALLOW DISH. PAT CHICKEN DRY WITH PAPER TOWELS, AND DIP IN BREADCRUMB MIXTURE, THEN IN EGGS, THEN BACK IN BREADCRUMB MIXTURE. LAY CHICKEN IN THE MELTED BUTTER AND BAKE 40 MINUTES.

MEANWHILE, MAKE SAUCE: IN A SMALL SAUCEPAN, MELT BUTTER OVER MEDIUM-LOW HEAT. STIR IN FLOUR. SLOWLY ADD MILK, AND COOK UNTIL THICKENED, STIRRING. ADD CHEESE AND STIR UNTIL MELTED.

TURN OVEN TO BROIL. SPOON CHEESE SAUCE OVER CHICKEN, AND BROIL UNTIL TOP IS LIGHTLY BROWNED.

KOZY KOUNTRY
BUTTERMILK PECAN CHICKEN
AND SUCH

SERVES 6

½ C. (1 STICK) BUTTER OR MARGARINE
1 C. BUTTERMILK
1 EGG, BEATEN
1½ C. GROUND PECANS
½ C. FLOUR
1½ tsp. SALT
6 CHICKEN BREAST HALVES

GO INTO A KITCHEN THAT HAS RUFFLED CURTAINS, AND WALLPAPER WITH LITTLE TEAKETTLES ALL OVER IT. PUT ON A GINGHAM APRON. PREHEAT OVEN TO 350°.

PUT BUTTER IN ROASTING PAN AND MELT IN OVEN, ABOUT 5 MINUTES. USING A POT HOLDER WITH A GOOSE WEARING A BLUE RIBBON AROUND IT'S NECK, REMOVE PAN AND SET ASIDE.

IN A SHALLOW DISH, WHISK BUTTERMILK AND EGG TOGETHER. IN ANOTHER SHALLOW DISH, PREFERABLY WITH DAISIES ON IT, COMBINE PECANS, FLOUR, AND SALT.

DIP CHICKEN IN BUTTERMILK MIXTURE, THEN COAT IN PECAN MIXTURE. PLACE IN THE ROASTING PAN, TURNING TO COAT WITH MELTED BUTTER. WIPE HANDS WITH TOWEL DECORATED WITH KITTENS PLAYING WITH A YARN BALL.

BAKE CHICKEN, UNCOVERED, 1 HOUR AND 10 MINUTES, OR UNTIL DEEP GOLDEN BROWN. ADD MORE BUTTER IF NECESSARY.

DECORATE THE TABLE WITH DRIED FLOWERS, DUCK NAPKIN HOLDERS, AND CORN HUSK DOLLS, AND SERVE.

DRUNKEN CHICKEN
CHICKEN PIECES, IMBIBED WITH A GOLDEN CHAMPAGNE SAUCE

SERVES 4

1	2 lb. FRYING CHICKEN
2	T. BUTTER OR MARGARINE
4	WHOLE GARLIC CLOVES, PEELED
1	PINCH EACH SALT AND PEPPER
1	BOTTLE DECENT CHAMPAGNE
1	T. CORNSTARCH DISSOLVED IN
	1½ T. COLD WATER

BUY A DEPRESSED CHICKEN. MAKE HIM EVEN MORE DEPRESSED BY CHOPPING HIM UP INTO SERVING PIECES. HEAT BUTTER IN A LARGE, DEEP SKILLET, AND LET HIM FRY IN HOT BUTTER OVER MEDIUM-HIGH HEAT UNTIL HE HAS A DEEP TAN. ADD GARLIC CLOVES AND A LITTLE SALT AND PEPPER.

KOCAR

TO MAKE CHICKEN GIGGLY, ADD 1 C. OF CHAMPAGNE TO SKILLET. COVER AND SIMMER 15 MINUTES.

TO MAKE CHICKEN DOWNRIGHT HAPPY, ADD ANOTHER CUP OF CHAMPAGNE. SIMMER AS BEFORE.

TO MAKE CHICKEN SLOPPY DRUNK, ADD ANOTHER CUP OF CHAMPAGNE. SIMMER AS BEFORE.

TO MAKE CHICKEN OBNOXIOUSLY ANNIHILATED, ADD THE LAST OF THE CHAMPAGNE. SIMMER AS BEFORE.

REMOVE CHICKEN FROM SKILLET, TAKE THE LAMPSHADE OFF HIS HEAD, AND LET HIM SOBER UP A LITTLE ON A WARMED PLATTER.

REMOVE GARLIC AND DISCARD. BOIL THE CHAMPAGNE 5-7 MINUTES UNTIL SLIGHTLY REDUCED. STIR IN THE CORNSTARCH MIXTURE TO THICKEN.

POUR SAUCE OVER RECOVERED CHICKEN, AND CRACK OPEN ANOTHER BOTTLE FOR YOURSELF.

CHOCOLATE CHICKEN

UNSWEETENED CHOCOLATE IS THE KEY INGREDIENT
TO THIS UNIQUE MEXICAN-INSPIRED RICH, BROWN SAUCE

SERVES 4

1/4	C. OLIVE OIL
4	CHICKEN BREAST HALVES, SKIN REMOVED
1/3	C. FLOUR
2	MEDIUM ONIONS, COARSELY CHOPPED
2	CLOVES GARLIC, MINCED
1	13 3/4 OZ. CAN CHICKEN BROTH
1/4	C. WHITE WINE
1	BAY LEAF
1/2	tsp. GROUND CINNAMON
1/2	tsp. CAYENNE PEPPER
1/2	tsp. SUGAR
1 1/2	tsp. SALT
3	T. TOMATO PASTE
1	SQUARE (1 OZ.) UNSWEETENED CHOCOLATE, FINELY CHOPPED
	RICE

HEAT OLIVE OIL IN LARGE SKILLET. DREDGE CHICKEN IN FLOUR, AND BROWN IN HOT OIL, ABOUT 7 MINUTES. REMOVE FROM SKILLET. ADD ONION AND GARLIC TO SKILLET, AND SAUTÉ 3 MINUTES OVER MEDIUM-HIGH HEAT. STIR IN CHICKEN BROTH, WINE, AND BAY LEAF. BRING TO A BOIL, RETURN CHICKEN, COVER, AND SIMMER 30 MINUTES. REMOVE CHICKEN TO WARM PLATTER. DISCARD BAY LEAF.

ADD CINNAMON, CAYENNE, SUGAR, SALT, AND TOMATO PASTE TO SKILLET. STIR UNTIL BLENDED. ADD CHOCOLATE LAST, STIRRING UNTIL MELTED

SERVE WITH COOKED RICE.

IF YOU'RE A CHOCOLATE CHICKEN LOVER, WAIT UNTIL YOU TRY MY LICORICE SOUP, SPLIT PEA TURNOVERS, CREAMED HERRING PANCAKES, AND GOOSELIVER SHERBET.

LIAR'S CHICKEN WELLINGTON
WITH CHEDDAR CHEESE SAUCE

EXTREMELY DIFFICULT TO PREPARE
SERVES 4

2	WHOLE BONELESS, SKINLESS CHICKEN BREASTS
1	3 OZ. PACKAGE CREAM CHEESE, SOFTENED
½	C. MAYONNAISE
1	tsp. SALT
1	8 OZ. TUBE CRESCENT ROLL DOUGH

SAUCE:	1	T. BUTTER OR MARGARINE
	1	T. FLOUR
	⅓	C. MILK
	⅔	C. GRATED CHEDDAR CHEESE

BOIL CHICKEN BREASTS UNTIL DONE, ABOUT 25 MINUTES. COOL SLIGHTLY. BREAK INTO SMALL PIECES IN MEDIUM BOWL.

WHAT YOU TELL YOUR GUESTS: YOU PURCHASED WHOLE, LIVE, FREE-RANGE CHICKENS FROM A NEARBY FARM TO INSURE FRESHNESS. YOU HAVE PLUCKING DOWN TO 10 MINUTES FLAT.

PREHEAT OVEN TO 375°. WITH A FORK, BLEND CREAM CHEESE, MAYONNAISE, AND SALT IN A MEDIUM BOWL. FOLD IN COOKED CHICKEN PIECES.

WHAT YOU TELL YOUR GUESTS: YOU INCLUDED 11 DIFFERENT EXOTIC SPICES IN THE FILLING. HAVE THEM GUESS AS MANY AS THEY CAN.

UNROLL THE DOUGH, AND SEPARATE INTO 4 RECTANGLES. FLATTEN SLIGHTLY TO MAKE A LITTLE MORE SQUARE, AND PINCH SEAMS TOGETHER. PLACE ¼ OF THE CHICKEN MIXTURE IN THE CENTER OF EACH SQUARE. BRING OPPOSITE CORNERS TOGETHER, AND PINCH CLOSED AT THE TOP. PINCH ALL SIDES CLOSED.

WHAT YOU TELL YOUR GUESTS: YOUR GREAT-GREAT-GREAT-GREAT GRANDMOTHER WAS THE PASTRY CHEF FOR KING JAMES I OF ENGLAND AND THIS WAS HER DOUGH RECIPE.

BAKE FOR 20 MINUTES OR UNTIL DEEP GOLDEN BROWN.

MEANWHILE MAKE CHEDDAR CHEESE SAUCE: IN A SMALL SAUCEPAN OVER MEDIUM HEAT, MELT BUTTER. STIR IN FLOUR. SLOWLY ADD MILK AND COOK, STIRRING, UNTIL THICKENED. ADD CHEESE AND STIR UNTIL MELTED. SPOON OVER CHICKEN WELLINGTONS.

WHAT YOU TELL YOUR GUESTS: YOU WARMED A CAN OF CHEDDAR CHEESE SOUP.

*CHIMP WITH BANANAS

A CARIBBEAN-INSPIRED TROPICAL DISH FOR EXOTIC PALATES.

SERVES 6

3	T. OLIVE OIL
2	T. BUTTER OR MARGARINE
2	lbs. BONELESS, SKINLESS CHICKEN BREASTS, CUT INTO BITE-SIZE PIECES
1	lb. RAW SHRIMP, PEELED AND DEVEINED
6	SCALLIONS, CHOPPED (WHITE PART ONLY)
2	CLOVES GARLIC, MINCED
2	T. FLOUR
1	13 3/4 OZ. CAN CHICKEN BROTH
1	BAY LEAF
1/4	tsp. GROUND MACE
1/4	tsp. CURRY POWDER
1 1/2	tsp. SALT
1/4	tsp. RED CAYENNE PEPPER
1	28 OZ. CAN CRUSHED TOMATOES, UNDRAINED
2	MEDIUM SWEET POTATOES, PEELED AND CUT INTO 1" CUBES
4	FIRM BANANAS
1 1/2	T. BUTTER OR MARGARINE

HEAT OIL AND BUTTER IN LARGE SKILLET AND SAUTÉ CHICKEN PIECES OVER HIGH HEAT UNTIL LIGHTLY BROWNED, ABOUT 5 MINUTES. REMOVE TO A PLATE. ADD SHRIMP TO SKILLET AND STIR FRY JUST UNTIL PINK, ABOUT 2 MINUTES. REMOVE TO PLATE WITH CHICKEN.

IF NECESSARY, ADD MORE BUTTER TO SKILLET AND SAUTÉ SCALLIONS AND GARLIC 1 MINUTE. STIR IN FLOUR. ADD CHICKEN BROTH, BAY LEAF, MACE, CURRY POWDER, SALT, CAYENNE, TOMATOES, AND SWEET POTATOES, AND MIX WELL. BRING TO A BOIL, TURN HEAT TO LOW, AND SIMMER 15 MINUTES, UNCOVERED.

REMOVE BAY LEAF. RETURN CHICKEN AND SHRIMP TO SKILLET, AND SIMMER 10 MORE MINUTES.

JUST BEFORE SERVING, SLICE BANANAS IN HALF WIDTHWISE AND THEN EACH HALF INTO THIRDS LENGTHWISE. HEAT BUTTER IN MEDIUM SKILLET, AND QUICKLY COOK BANANAS OVER HIGH HEAT UNTIL LIGHTLY BROWNED BUT NOT TOO SOFT.

TO SERVE, ARRANGE BANANAS AROUND CHIMP.

* CHIMP = CHICKEN + SHRIMP

HUHN IM TOPF FLEISCHKLOESSCHEN MIT SPAETZLES

A WONDERFUL GERMAN STEW OF CHICKEN AND MEATBALLS IN A POT
WITH SPAETZLES INSPIRED BY MY FRIEND KURT BÖHM

SERVES 8

- 8 BONELESS, SKINLESS CHICKEN THIGHS
- 6 CARROTS, SCRAPED AND CUT INTO ½" CHUNKS
- 2 MEDIUM ONIONS, COARSELY CHOPPED
- 1 13¾ OZ. CAN CHICKEN BROTH
- 2 BAY LEAVES
- 1 T. DRIED PARSLEY LEAVES
- 1 lb. GROUND SIRLOIN
- ½ lb. GROUND PORK
- ⅓ C. DRY BREADCRUMBS
- 1 EGG
- 2 CLOVES GARLIC, MINCED
- 1 tsp. SALT
- ½ tsp. PEPPER
- 1 10½ OZ. BOX SPAETZLE NOODLES

GERMAN RYE BREAD

PLACE CHICKEN IN A DEEP POT ALONG WITH CARROTS AND ONIONS. ADD CHICKEN BROTH AND ENOUGH WATER TO COVER. ADD BAY LEAVES AND PARSLEY. BRING TO A BOIL AND SIMMER FOR 30 MINUTES UNCOVERED.

MEANWHILE MAKE MEATBALLS. IN A LARGE BOWL, COMBINE GROUND MEATS WITH BREADCRUMBS EGG GARLIC SALT AND PEPPER. MIX WITH HANDS AND FORM SMALL MEATBALLS. ADD TO THE CHICKEN AND SIMMER 20 MINUTES MORE UNCOVERED.

WHILE MEATBALLS ARE COOKING, PREPARE SPAETZLES ACCORDING TO PACKAGE DIRECTIONS. DRAIN AND ADD TO CHICKEN.

REMOVE BAY LEAVES.

SERVE STEW WITH CHUNKS OF GERMAN RYE BREAD.

POLISH PASTA

A DELICIOUS, GARLICKY STIR-FRY WITH KIELBASA
AND CHICKEN THAT TAKES 6 PEOPLE TO PREPARE:
1 TO HOLD THE SPOON AND 5 TO ROCK THE STOVE.

SERVES 4

1	C. UNCOOKED DITALINI (SMALL, TUBULAR PASTA)
1/3	C. BUTTER OR MARGARINE
2	WHOLE BONELESS, SKINLESS CHICKEN BREASTS, CUT INTO BITE-SIZE PIECES
1	MEDIUM ONION, CHOPPED
1/2	C. CHOPPED SCALLIONS (INCLUDE SOME GREENS)
1	PRECOOKED POLISH KIELBASA (ABOUT 12" LONG), SLICED INTO ROUNDS
4	CLOVES GARLIC, MINCED
1 1/4	C. WHITE WINE

SALT AND PEPPER TO TASTE

BOIL DITALINI UNTIL TENDER.
RINSE IN COLD WATER, DRAIN,
AND SET ASIDE.

MELT BUTTER IN LARGE SKILLET,
AND LIGHTLY BROWN CHICKEN
PIECES OVER MEDIUM-HIGH
HEAT.

ADD ONION AND SCALLIONS
AND STIR-FRY 4 MINUTES.
ADD KIELBASA AND GARLIC,
AND COOK 3 MORE MINUTES,
STIRRING.

STIR IN WINE AND DITALINI
AND HEAT THROUGH.

SERVE IMMEDIATELY.

THIS DISH WILL GUARANTEE
RAVES AND HALITOSIS.

KOCAR

GORMAY PEETSA
WITH CHICKEN, PISTACHIOS, AND PESTO
SERVES 4

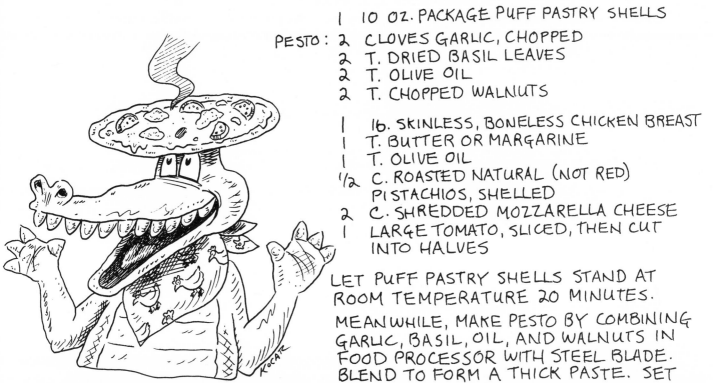

1	10 OZ.	PACKAGE PUFF PASTRY SHELLS
PESTO:	2	CLOVES GARLIC, CHOPPED
	2	T. DRIED BASIL LEAVES
	2	T. OLIVE OIL
	2	T. CHOPPED WALNUTS
1	1b.	SKINLESS, BONELESS CHICKEN BREAST
1	T.	BUTTER OR MARGARINE
1	T.	OLIVE OIL
1/2	C.	ROASTED NATURAL (NOT RED) PISTACHIOS, SHELLED
2	C.	SHREDDED MOZZARELLA CHEESE
1		LARGE TOMATO, SLICED, THEN CUT INTO HALVES

LET PUFF PASTRY SHELLS STAND AT ROOM TEMPERATURE 20 MINUTES.

MEANWHILE, MAKE PESTO BY COMBINING GARLIC, BASIL, OIL, AND WALNUTS IN FOOD PROCESSOR WITH STEEL BLADE. BLEND TO FORM A THICK PASTE. SET ASIDE.

ON LIGHTLY FLOURED SURFACE, STACK PASTRY SHELLS ON TOP OF EACH OTHER, PRESS DOWN, AND WITH A ROLLING PIN, FLATTEN TO A 12" ROUND. LET STAND 15 MINUTES.

PREHEAT OVEN TO 450°.

CUT CHICKEN INTO SMALL PIECES. HEAT BUTTER AND OIL IN MEDIUM SKILLET AND SAUTÉ CHICKEN UNTIL LIGHTLY BROWNED, ABOUT 5-7 MINUTES. SET ASIDE.

BAKE PASTRY ROUND ON UNGREASED COOKIE SHEET 10 MINUTES. REMOVE FROM OVEN, CUT A FEW SLITS TO VENT, AND PRESS GENTLY TO FLATTEN.

ASSEMBLE PEETSA: WITH RUBBER SPATULA, SPREAD PESTO ON PASTRY. TOP WITH CHICKEN AND PISTACHIOS. COVER WITH CHEESE.

BAKE 5 MINUTES OR UNTIL CHEESE MELTS. ARRANGE TOMATO PIECES ON TOP. BROIL 2 MINUTES MORE.

CUT INTO 4 PIECES.

ADOBO ROMEO
SAVORY GINGER PORK STEW

ROMEO, A SURGEON FRIEND FROM THE PHILLIPINES, TAUGHT ME HOW TO MAKE THIS NATIONAL DISH OF HIS HOMELAND. HIS SKILL WITH A KNIFE WAS SO IMPRESSIVE, I HAVE YET TO SEE A PROFESSIONAL CHEF WITH MORE SPEED OR ACCURACY. HE CAN OPERATE ON ME ANY TIME.

SERVES 4

1	3½-4 lb. BONELESS PORK LOIN ROAST
½	C. SOY SAUCE
½	C. BOTTLED TERIYAKI SAUCE
1	LARGE ONION, COARSELY CHOPPED
3	CLOVES GARLIC, MINCED
¼	C. COARSELY CHOPPED GINGER ROOT
1	T. SUGAR
2	tsp. INSTANT CHICKEN BOUILLON
½	C. WHITE VINEGAR
1	tsp. SALT
1	tsp. PEPPER

COOKED WHITE RICE

KOCAR

TRIM FAT FROM PORK AND SLICE PORK INTO ½" THICK SLICES. PLACE IN LARGE POT. ADD THE REST OF THE INGREDIENTS EXCEPT THE RICE. POUR IN ENOUGH WATER TO COVER MEAT. BRING TO A BOIL, AND OVER MEDIUM-LOW HEAT, SIMMER 1½ HOURS, UNCOVERED.

WITH A SLOTTED SPOON, REMOVE PORK TO A SERVING DISH. STRAIN SAUCE THROUGH A SIEVE, AND PASS SEPARATELY.

SERVE WITH A MOUND OF GOOD WHITE RICE.

LIZZIE BORDEN PORK CHOP STEW
A SIMPLE, YET PENETRATING DISH

SERVES 6: YOUR FATHER, YOUR STEP-MOTHER, AND
4 OTHER WARM-BLOODED GUESTS

6	½" THICK RIB PORK CHOPS
⅓	C. FLOUR
1	tsp. SALT
½	tsp. PEPPER
1	tsp. RED CAYENNE PEPPER
2	T. OLIVE OIL
1	10¾ OZ. CAN CHICKEN BROTH
2	T. BOTTLED STEAK SAUCE
¼	C. DRY RED WINE
3	ONIONS
6	CARROTS
6	POTATOES

TAKE AN AX. WHACK EXCESS FAT FROM CHOPS. IN A SHALLOW DISH, COMBINE FLOUR, SALT, AND PEPPERS. COAT CHOPS WELL, AND RESERVE REMAINING FLOUR MIXTURE.

HEAT OIL IN LARGE SKILLET, AND BROWN CHOPS ON BOTH SIDES. REMOVE FROM SKILLET AND SET ASIDE.

IN SAME SKILLET, STIR IN RESERVED FLOUR MIXTURE. ADD BROTH, STEAK SAUCE, AND RED WINE. SIMMER OVER MEDIUM-LOW HEAT 3 MINUTES, STIRRING CONSTANTLY. REMOVE FROM HEAT.

PREHEAT OVEN TO 350°.

CARVE ONIONS INTO THIN SLICES. TRUNCATE THE TOPS OF THE CARROTS AND HACK CARROTS INTO 1" PIECES. CLEAVE THE POTATOES INTO ½" SLICES.

IN LARGE CASSEROLE DISH, LAYER HALF THE VEGETABLES. ADD BROWNED CHOPS. ARRANGE REMAINING VEGETABLES ON TOP. POUR BROTH MIXTURE OVER.

BAKE 2 HOURS, COVERED.

CHINESE BABY BACK RIBS
SERVES 6

1/4 C. SOY SAUCE	1/4 C. BOTTLED HOISIN SAUCE	1/4 C. DRY SHERRY	1/4 C. HONEY	1/4 C. KETCHUP	3 CLOVES GARLIC, MINCED	1 tsp. GRATED FRESH GINGER	1 tsp. SALT	1/2 tsp. PEPPER	4 lbs. BABY BACK PORK RIBS

WHISK FIRST 9 INGREDIENTS TOGETHER IN A MEDIUM BOWL TO BLEND.

PUT RIBS IN LARGE ROASTING PAN,

POUR MARINADE OVER, AND REFRIGERATE AT LEAST 3 HOURS.

PREHEAT OVEN TO 350°.

POUR OFF HALF

THE MARINADE, RESERVE, AND BAKE RIBS 30 MINUTES. IF LIQUID STARTS TO DRY, ADD A LITTLE WATER.

TURN RIBS, ADD REST OF MARINADE, AND BAKE ANOTHER 35 MINUTES, BASTING OCCASIONALLY.

SERVE IMMEDIATELY.

KOCAR

PIT BULL BURGERS

A DIFFERENT AND DOGGONE GOOD HAMBURGER
THAT SHOULD BE GRILLED

SERVES 4 - 6

2	lbs. GROUND PIT BULL OR GROUND SIRLOIN
2/3	C. CHOPPED PIT BULL BONES OR WALNUTS
2	HANDFULS OF FINE DRY BREADCRUMBS
1	FISTFUL OF FRESHLY GRATED PARMESAN CHEESE
1	HEARTY SPLASH OF DRY SHERRY
1	tsp. SALT
1/2	tsp. FRESHLY GROUND BLACK PEPPER
	ROLLS OR BUNS

IN A LARGE BOWL, MIX ALL INGREDIENTS EXCEPT ROLLS.
FORM INTO BURGERS, AND GRILL AS DESIRED. PLACE ON
ROLL AND TOP WITH GARNISH OF YOUR CHOICE.

SINK TEETH INTO.

SUGGESTION: USE ITALIAN OR FRENCH ROLLS, LIGHTLY
TOASTED, AND SHAPE THE BURGER TO FIT THE BUN.

MY MOTHER-IN-LAW'S MEATLOAF

2 lbs. FATTY GROUND BEEF, LACED WITH
    GRISTLE, PARTIALLY FROZEN
SALT AND PEPPER

PREHEAT OVEN TO BROIL. PAT GROUND
BEEF INTO A GLOB. SPRINKLE WITH
SALT AND PEPPER. BROIL UNTIL TOP
IS CHARRED AND DRY AND MIDDLE IS
STILL PARTIALLY FROZEN. DON'T
BOTHER DRAINING FAT.

SERVE WITH INSTANT POTATO FLAKES.

KOCAR

MY MEATLOAF

SERVES 6

1	lb. GROUND TURKEY
1	lb. GROUND CHUCK
1	C. SEASONED DRY BREAD CRUMBS
1/4	C. GRATED PARMESAN CHEESE
1/3	C. KETCHUP
2	EGGS
2	T. WORCESTERSHIRE SAUCE
1	SMALL ONION, FINELY CHOPPED
2	CLOVES GARLIC, MINCED
1	6 OZ. CAN TOMATO PASTE
4	SLICES SHARP CHEDDAR CHEESE

PREHEAT OVEN TO 375°. PUT FIRST NINE INGREDIENTS IN
LARGE BOWL. MIX WELL WITH HANDS. PRESS INTO
APPROPRIATELY SIZED LOAF PAN. SPREAD TOMATO PASTE
OVER TOP. BAKE FOR 1 HOUR AND 10 MINUTES.

SPREAD CHEDDAR CHEESE SLICES ON TOP OF MEATLOAF
AND BAKE ANOTHER 5-7 MINUTES, OR UNTIL CHEESE
IS MELTED.

SERVE WITH CHILLED 1787 CHÂTEAU LAFITE.

MOO MOO FRY PAN
CHINESE BEEF IN A SKILLET WITH CASHEWS

SERVES 4

1 lb. BEEF SIRLOIN, CUT INTO STRIPS
2 tsp. BUTTER OR MARGARINE
2 tsp. OLIVE OIL
4 SCALLIONS, SLICED (INCLUDE SOME GREENS)
1 8 OZ. CAN SLICED BAMBOO SHOOTS, DRAINED
1 tsp. FRESHLY GRATED GINGER
1/2 tsp. SALT
1/4 tsp. PEPPER
1 13 3/4 OZ. CAN BEEF BROTH
2 T. CORNSTARCH DISSOLVED IN 3 T. COLD WATER
1/2 HEAD CHINESE CABBAGE, COARSELY CHOPPED
3/4 C. WHOLE SALTED CASHEWS
COOKED WHITE OR BROWN RICE

PAT BEEF DRY WITH PAPER TOWELS. HEAT BUTTER AND OIL IN LARGE SKILLET, AND BROWN BEEF STRIPS ON HIGH HEAT ABOUT 5 MINUTES. LOWER HEAT TO MEDIUM, AND STIR IN SCALLIONS, BAMBOO SHOOTS, GINGER, SALT, AND PEPPER. COOK 1 MINUTE. POUR BEEF BROTH ALL OVER, BRING TO A SIMMER, ADD DISSOLVED CORNSTARCH, AND STIR UNTIL THICKENED.

ADD CABBAGE AND CASHEWS, AND STIR-FRY 2-3 MINUTES. SERVE IMMEDIATELY OVER RICE.

KOCAR

A ROAST CALLED RICK

SERVES 6

1	8 OZ. JAR PREPARED BROWN MUSTARD
2	CLOVES GARLIC, MINCED
2	tsp. BLACK PEPPER, DIVIDED
1	T. BROWN SUGAR
1	3 lb. BONELESS EYE OF ROUND BEEF ROAST NAMED RICK
1½	lbs. (APPROX.) COARSE SALT
2	T. BUTTER OR MARGARINE
1	C. CHOPPED MUSHROOMS
½	C. DRY RED WINE
1	tsp. INSTANT BEEF BOUILLON

ONE DAY RICK PREHEATED THE OVEN TO 325°. HE THEN MIXED THE MUSTARD, GARLIC, 1 tsp. BLACK PEPPER, AND BROWN SUGAR IN A SMALL BOWL. WITH A RUBBER SPATULA, HE COVERED HIS TOP AND SIDES WITH THE MUSTARD MIXTURE, SAVING HIS BOTTOM FOR LAST.

THEN RICK ROLLED AROUND AND AROUND IN THE COARSE SALT, COATING HIMSELF COMPLETELY AND THOROUGHLY UNTIL THERE WAS NO PLACE LEFT TO PEEK.

HE ROASTED FOR 1 HOUR IN A ROASTING PAN AT 325°, AND FOR ANOTHER HOUR AT 250°.

THEN RICK TOOK A 20 MINUTE REST.

AFTER REPOSING, HE BROKE THROUGH HIS JACKET OF SALT AND DISCARDED EVERY LAST PIECE. HE SLICED HIMSELF INTO THIN SLICES.

IN A LARGE SKILLET, RICK HEATED THE BUTTER AND SAUTÉED THE MUSHROOMS OVER MEDIUM-HIGH HEAT 3 MINUTES. THEN HE ADDED THE WINE, REMAINING BLACK PEPPER, AND BEEF BOUILLON. WHEN EVERYTHING WAS SIMMERING NICELY, RICK AND HIS SLICES JUMPED IN FOR A 5 MINUTE BATH BEFORE BEING SERVED.

RICK LIVED HAPPILY EVER AFTER IN THE HEARTS AND STOMACHS OF 6 VERY SATISFIED PEOPLE.

KOCAR

HOLY COW
BEEF TENDERLOIN WITH THYME

A RELIGIOUS EXPERIENCE THAT SERVETHS A CONGREGATION OF 4

2 lbs. BEEF TENDERLOIN
4 T. BUTTER
2 ONIONS, CHOPPED
2 CLOVES GARLIC, MINCED
2 T. TOMATO PASTE
2 T. FLOUR
1 C. BEEF BROTH
2/3 C. DRY RED WINE
JUICE OF 1 LEMON
1 tsp. GROUND THYME
SALT AND PEPPER TO TASTE

GO UNTO THE KITCHEN AND LAY THINE HAND UPON A SHARP KNIFE. CAST IT UPON THE BEEF TENDERLOIN, SLICING IT INTO STRIPS. IN A LARGE SKILLET, THOU SHALT SAUTÉ IT IN THE BUTTER OVER HIGH HEAT UNTIL LIGHTLY BROWNED, ABOUT 7 MINUTES.

LET THERE BE LOWER HEAT, STIR IN ONION AND GARLIC AND SAUTÉTH 3 MINUTES. STIRETH IN TOMATO PASTE, THEN SPRINKLETH IN FLOUR. GO FORTH AND TOSS THE MEAT UNTIL COATED.

BEHOLD THE BROTH AND WINE, ADD TO THINE SKILLET, AND STIRETH TO MAKETH A SMOOTH SAUCE. YEA, THAT YOU MAY SQUEEZETH THE LEMON OVER THE MEAT AND BLENDETH IN THE THYME. COOK A FEW MINUTES MORE, I PRAY THEE, AND SALT AND PEPPER TO TASTE.

BEHOLD THE FRUITS OF THY LABORS WHICH THOU HAST SOWN.

SERVETH WITH MASHED POTATOES, UNLEVENED BREAD, AND A FLAGON OF WINE.

AMEN.

BEEF TIPS

1. STAY AWAY FROM GREEN MEAT.
2. DON'T COOK IT IF IT'S STILL MOOING.
3. DON'T ATTEMPT TO MELT IT.
4. REMOVE HIDE BEFORE SERVING.
5. TRY THIS DELECTABLE RECIPE FOR BEEF TIPS AND RED POTATOES IN A SHALLOT VERMOUTH SAUCE.

SERVES 4-6

1 1/2	lbs. RED POTATOES
1/4	C. (1/2 STICK) SWEET BUTTER
1	2 1/2 lb. BONELESS SIRLOIN TIP ROAST, CUT INTO 1" PIECES
4	T. BUTTER OR MARGARINE
1/2	C. FINELY CHOPPED SHALLOTS
1	C. DRY WHITE VERMOUTH
1	C. CHICKEN BROTH
1	TSP. SALT
1/2	tsp. GROUND WHITE PEPPER
3	T. SOFTENED BUTTER OR MARGARINE, MASHED WITH 3 T. FLOUR
1/3	C. FINELY CHOPPED FRESH PARSLEY

WASH AND QUARTER RED POTATOES. PUT IN SAUCEPAN WITH STEAMER AND 1" WATER, AND STEAM JUST UNTIL FORK TENDER, ABOUT 12 MINUTES. SET ASIDE.

MEANWHILE, CLARIFY BUTTER BY MELTING IN SMALL SAUCEPAN OVER LOW HEAT. COOL AND SKIM FOAM FROM SURFACE. DISCARD FOAM.

IN LARGE SKILLET OVER HIGH HEAT, BROWN SIRLOIN PIECES IN CLARIFIED BUTTER. POUR OFF EXCESS JUICES ACCUMULATED WHILE COOKING, AND RESERVE. REMOVE MEAT.

IN SAME SKILLET, MELT 4 T. BUTTER AND COOK SHALLOTS OVER LOW HEAT UNTIL SOFT, BUT NOT BROWNED. ADD WINE, BROTH, SALT, AND PEPPER, AND SIMMER 5 MINUTES. ADD BUTTER AND FLOUR MIXTURE, A LITTLE AT A TIME, STIRRING CONSTANTLY. CONTINUE STIRRING UNTIL SAUCE IS SMOOTH. RETURN BEEF AND RESERVED JUICES TO SKILLET, BLEND, AND ADD RED POTATOES.

SIMMER, UNCOVERED 15-20 MINUTES. JUST BEFORE SERVING, ADD PARSLEY.

6. IF YOU'RE A COW, LEARN HOW TO BARK.

VEAL LEGALESE
VEAL IN LEMON-PEPPER BATTER

SERVES 4

4   LARGE VEAL STEAKS
4   EGGS
2   LEMONS
FLOUR
2   tsp. COARSELY GROUND BLACK PEPPER
3   T. BUTTER OR MARGARINE
3   T. VEGETABLE OIL

1   LEMON, SLICED, FOR GARNISH

WHEREAS, THE PARTY OF THE FIRST PART HEREBY COVENANTS TO PREPARE FOR THE PARTY OF THE MOST PART THE AFOREMENTIONED MAIN COURSE USING THOSE INGREDIENTS SET FORTH HEREINABOVE;

NOW, THEREFORE, IN CONSIDERATION OF A HEARTY APPETITE AND OTHER VALUABLE CONSIDERATION THE PARTIES HERETO AGREE THAT THE PARTY OF THE FIRST PART SHALL PROCEED AS FOLLOWS:

PREAMBLE. PREHEAT OVEN TO LOWEST TEMPERATURE. PREPARE VEAL BY POUNDING THIN WITH GAVEL AND CUTTING INTO MEDALLIONS AS IF CROSS-EXAMINING THE DEFENDANT.

BEAT EGGS IN A MEDIUM BOWL AND STIR IN JUICE FROM 1 1/2 LEMONS. BLEND IN ENOUGH FLOUR TO MAKE A SEMI-RUNNY, SEMI-FIRM BATTER. STIR IN PEPPER.

HEAT BUTTER AND OIL IN LARGE SKILLET. DIP VEAL IN LEMON-PEPPER BATTER AS SET FORTH IN SUBPARAGRAPH 2, HEREINABOVE, AND FRY A FEW PIECES AT A TIME OVER MEDIUM HEAT IPSO FACTO, UNTIL GOLDEN, TURNING ONCE (ABOUT 5-7 MINUTES). AS THEY ARE DONE, REMOVE TO OVEN-PROOF SERVING PLATTER, AND KEEP WARM IN OVEN. TIME IS OF THE ESSENCE.

ADD JUICE FROM 1/2 LEMON TO PAN JUICES. COOK, STIRRING, ABOUT 3 MINUTES PRO TANTO UNTIL SKILLET IS DEGLAZED. ANYTHING TO THE CONTRARY HEREIN NOTWITHSTANDING, POUR LEMON SAUCE OVER VEAL.

CLOSING ARGUMENT. GARNISH WITH LEMON SLICES QUANTUM MERUIT. YOU MAY REST YOUR CASE AND WAIT FOR THE JUDGES TO RULE IN YOUR FLAVOR.

TURF AND TURF ON THE GRILL

A WONDERFUL PAIRING OF ROSEMARY-LACED LAMB CHOPS WITH MINT JELLY AND BLACK PEPPER-BOURBON STEAK TENDERLOIN WITH BÉARNAISE SAUCE.

SERVES 4

¼ C. OLIVE OIL
1 T. ROSEMARY LEAVES, CRUSHED
2 CLOVES GARLIC, MINCED
2 tsp. FRESH LEMON JUICE
1 tsp. SALT
½ tsp. GROUND WHITE PEPPER
8 SINGLE RIB LOIN LAMB CHOPS, 1" THICK
MINT JELLY

IN A SMALL BOWL, COMBINE OIL, ROSEMARY, GARLIC, LEMON, SALT, AND PEPPER. BRUSH ON BOTH SIDES OF THE LAMB CHOPS.

¼ C. BOURBON WHISKEY
3 T. FRESHLY GROUND BLACK PEPPER
1½ lb. STEAK TENDERLOIN, CUT INTO 4 1" THICK STEAKS

BÉARNAISE:
2 T. WHITE WINE
1 T. DRIED TARRAGON LEAVES
2 tsp. FINELY CHOPPED SHALLOTS
3 EGG YOLKS
2 T. FRESH LEMON JUICE
¼ tsp. SALT
½ C. (1 STICK) HOT MELTED BUTTER OR MARGARINE

PLACE BOURBON IN ONE SHALLOW BOWL, AND PEPPER IN ANOTHER. DIP EACH STEAK IN THE BOURBON, AND THEN COAT WITH PEPPER.

PREPARE MEATS AS ABOVE. OVER A MEDIUM-HOT GRILL, COOK LAMB CHOPS AND STEAKS AT THE SAME TIME, ABOUT 5 MINUTES PER SIDE.

MEANWHILE, MAKE BÉARNAISE SAUCE: IN A SMALL SKILLET, COMBINE WINE, TARRAGON, AND SHALLOTS. BOIL UNTIL LIQUID IS GONE BUT MIXTURE IS STILL MOIST. IN A BLENDER, MIX TOGETHER EGG YOLKS, LEMON, SALT, AND TARRAGON-SHALLOT MIXTURE. WITH BLENDER ON HIGH, VERY SLOWLY DRIZZLE HOT BUTTER IN UNTIL SAUCE IS CREAMY AND THICKENED. (IF SAUCE NEEDS MORE THICKENING, MICROWAVE ON LOW A FEW SECONDS AT A TIME AND STIR.)

SERVE EACH PERSON 2 LAMB CHOPS WITH MINT JELLY AND 1 STEAK WITH BÉARNAISE SAUCE.

MARY HAD A LITTLE LAMB CHOP
SERVES 4

MARY HAD A LITTLE LAMB, LITTLE LAMB, LITTLE LAMB.
MARY HAD A LITTLE LAMB. IT'S FLEECE WAS WHITE
AS SNOW. IT FOLLOWED HER TO SCHOOL ONE DAY,
WHICH WAS AGAINST THE RULE, SO SHE SLAUGHTERED
IT.

    1/2 C. (1 STICK) SWEET BUTTER
    2/3 C. WHOLE, BLANCHED ALMONDS
    2/3 C. WALNUTS
    4   SLICES ITALIAN BREAD, CRUSTS REMOVED
    12   SINGLE RIB LOIN LAMB CHOPS, 3/4" THICK
    FLOUR FOR DREDGING
    4   EGGS, BEATEN
    SALT AND PEPPER TO TASTE

CLARIFY BUTTER BY MELTING IN SMALL SAUCEPAN OVER
LOW HEAT, COOLING, AND SKIMMING FOAM FROM SURFACE.
DISCARD FOAM.

IN FOOD PROCESSOR WITH STEEL BLADE, FINELY CHOP ALMONDS
AND WALNUTS. TRANSFER TO MEDIUM BOWL. PROCESS BREAD
TO FINE CRUMBS, AND COMBINE WITH NUTS.

PREHEAT OVEN TO LOWEST TEMPERATURE.

DREDGE LAMB CHOPS IN FLOUR, DIP IN BEATEN EGGS, AND
COAT WELL WITH NUT MIXTURE.

IN LARGE, HEAVY SKILLET, HEAT CLARIFIED BUTTER AND
COOK LAMB CHOPS, A FEW AT A TIME, OVER MEDIUM-HIGH
HEAT ABOUT 5 MINUTES PER SIDE FOR MEDIUM. DRAIN ON
PAPER TOWELS, PLACE IN ROASTING PAN, AND KEEP WARM
IN OVEN UNTIL ALL ARE COOKED. SPRINKLE GENEROUSLY
WITH SALT AND PEPPER. SERVE 3 LAMB CHOPS TO EACH
PERSON.

KOCAR

YOU ARE NOT LEAVING THIS TABLE UNTIL YOU FINISH YOUR LIMA BEANS (AND ITALIAN SAUSAGE SKILLET)

SERVES 6

3 lbs. ITALIAN SWEET SAUSAGE IN CASINGS
1 BOTTLE DRY WHITE WINE
2 T. OLIVE OIL
2 ONIONS, COARSELY CHOPPED
4 CLOVES GARLIC, COARSELY CHOPPED
2 LARGE TOMATOES, PEELED AND COARSELY CHOPPED
1 tsp. FRESHLY GROUND PEPPER
1 BAY LEAF
1 tsp. DRIED BASIL
2 tsp. SUGAR
1/2 C. CHICKEN BROTH
2 10 OZ. PACKAGES FROZEN BABY LIMA BEANS, THAWED
SALT TO TASTE
6 POTATOES, PEELED AND QUARTERED
1/4 C. (1/2 STICK) BUTTER OR MARGARINE
1/4 C. MILK

PLACE SAUSAGES IN LARGE, HEAVY SKILLET. POUR IN ENOUGH WINE TO ALMOST COVER, AND COOK OVER MEDIUM HEAT, UNCOVERED, UNTIL WINE IS COOKED DOWN, ABOUT 20 MINUTES. BROWN SAUSAGES EVENLY. TRANSFER TO PLATE AND CUT INTO 1" PIECES.

IN SAME SKILLET, ADD OLIVE OIL, HEAT, AND SAUTÉ ONION AND GARLIC UNTIL GOLDEN, ABOUT 3 MINUTES. STIR IN TOMATOES, PEPPER, BAY LEAF, BASIL, AND SUGAR. COOK 5 MINUTES.

RETURN SAUSAGES TO SKILLET AND ADD CHICKEN BROTH, 1/2 C. MORE WHITE WINE, AND LIMA BEANS. COVER AND SIMMER 45 MINUTES.

MEANWHILE, BOIL POTATOES UNTIL TENDER, DRAIN, AND WITH ELECTRIC MIXER, MASH WITH BUTTER AND MILK. SERVE WITH SAUSAGE DISH, SPOONING SAUCE OVER.

SIT DOWN. PUT YOUR NAPKIN IN YOUR LAP. QUIT SCOWLING. SIT UP STRAIGHT. HOLD YOUR FORK PROPERLY. GET YOUR ELBOWS OFF THE TABLE.

NOW ENJOY, GODDAMN IT.

BEST WURST
BERLIN·STYLE BRATWURST WITH MASHED POTATOES
SERVES 4-6

12 BRATWURST
3 T. BUTTER OR MARGARINE
2 MEDIUM ONIONS, THINLY SLICED
1½ C. BEER (12 OZ.), ROOM TEMPERATURE
2 BAY LEAVES
1½ tsp. SALT
¼ tsp. GROUND WHITE PEPPER
½ tsp. SUGAR
4 LARGE POTATOES, PEELED AND CUT INTO CHUNKS
3 T. BUTTER OR MARGARINE
3 T. MILK
2 T. FLOUR MIXED WITH 3 T. COLD WATER

PLACE BRATWURST IN LARGE SKILLET, AND COVER WITH WATER. BRING TO A BOIL, AND COOK 5 MINUTES. POUR WATER OFF AND IN SAME SKILLET, ADD BUTTER, AND BROWN BRATWURST OVER MEDIUM HEAT. REMOVE TO A PLATE.

ADD ONIONS TO SKILLET, AND COOK, STIRRING, 3 MINUTES. RETURN BRATWURST, AND ADD BEER, BAY LEAVES, SALT, PEPPER, AND SUGAR. SIMMER, UNCOVERED, 15 MINUTES.

MEANWHILE, MAKE MASHED POTATOES: PLACE POTATO CHUNKS IN A LARGE SAUCEPAN, COVER WITH WATER, AND BOIL UNTIL TENDER, 12-15 MINUTES. DRAIN, ADD BUTTER AND MILK, AND MASH WITH ELECTRIC MIXER. SET ASIDE.

REMOVE BRATWURST TO A PLATE AGAIN, AND STIR FLOUR MIXTURE INTO BEER SAUCE. COOK OVER MEDIUM HEAT, STIRRING, 3 MINUTES, OR UNTIL THICKENED. REMOVE BAY LEAVES.

RETURN BRATWURST TO SKILLET AND WARM. REHEAT POTATOES AT THE SAME TIME.

SERVE BRATWURST OVER POTATOES, AND SPOON BEER SAUCE OVER.

STEAMED RED CABBAGE IS A NICE ACCOMPANIMENT.

MY FATHER-IN-LAW'S FETTUCINI CARBONARA

2 OZ. GIN
SPLASH OF VERMOUTH
1 ANCHOVY-STUFFED GREEN OLIVE

COMBINE INGREDIENTS IN CHILLED MARTINI GLASS. ORDER OUT FOR CHINESE.

MY FETTUCINI CARBONARA

SERVES 4-6

1 lb. FETTUCINI NOODLES
2 T. OLIVE OIL
1/2 lb. CANADIAN BACON, JULIENNED
6 SCALLIONS, SLICED (INCLUDE A LITTLE GREEN)
1/3 C. PINE NUTS
1/2 C. (1 STICK) HOT, MELTED BUTTER OR MARGARINE
1/2 C. FRESHLY GRATED PARMESAN CHEESE
1/2 tsp. DRIED OREGANO
SALT AND COARSELY GROUND PEPPER TO TASTE
3 EGGS, BEATEN
CHOPPED FRESH PARSLEY FOR GARNISH

COOK FETTUCINI ACCORDING TO PACKAGE DIRECTIONS. MEANWHILE, IN LARGE SKILLET, HEAT OLIVE OIL. SAUTÉ BACON 3 MINUTES. ADD SCALLIONS AND PINE NUTS AND STIR FRY 2 MINUTES OVER MEDIUM HEAT.

DRAIN FETTUCINI AND ADD TO SKILLET. TURN HEAT TO VERY LOW, ADD BUTTER, CHEESE, OREGANO, SALT, AND PEPPER, AND TOSS GENTLY UNTIL HEATED THROUGH. AT THE VERY LAST MINUTE, ADD EGGS AND TOSS AGAIN.

SERVE ON WARMED PLATES.

GARNISH WITH PARSLEY.

TWO-LEGGED BART'S SPAGHETTI WESTERN

DANG GOOD VITTLES WITH ENUFFIN KICK
TO LIFT YA PLUM OUTA YER SADDLE

MAKES 'BOUT 12 PUNCHERS FULL AS A TICK ON A BUFFLER

2	lbs. FRESH GROUND TURKEY
3	T. OLIVE OIL
1	48 OZ. JAR OF YER FAVORITE STORE-BOUGHT SPAGHETTI SAUCE
1	12 OZ. CAN TOMATER PASTE
1	28 OZ. CAN CRUSHED TOMATERS
1	16 OZ. CAN RED KIDNEY BEANS
*1	4 OZ. CAN JALEPEÑO PEPPERS, DRAINED AND CHOPPED ALL UP
2	tsp. SUGAR
2	T. INSTANT BEEF BOULLION
2	CLOVES GARLIC, CRUSHED ALL UP

THEM THIN TYPE SPAGHETTI NOODLES
LONGHORN COLBY CHEESE, GRATED

RUSTLE UP A MEDIUM TYPE SKILLET, AND BROWN UP THAT THAR TURKEY MEAT IN THE OIL TILL IT'S ALL NICE AND COOKED UP; 'BOUT THE COLOR OF A PRAIRIE DOG. SIT ASIDE.

GIT YERSELF A BIG OLE POT, ROUND UP ALL THE REST OF THEM THAR GREDIENTS (CEPTIN' FER THE LAST 2), AND TOSS 'EM IN. HEAT EVERTHIN' UP TILL IT'S ASIMMERIN' LIKE A CRICK DURIN' THE GOLD RUSH. DON'T FERGIT TA THROW IN THAT GOBBLER MEAT.

COOK 'ER UP ON A LOW FIRE, WITHOUTIN' NO COVER, FER 'BOUT HALF AN HOUR, TILL SHE'S BUBBLIN', AN THICK AS BUNKHOUSE COFFEE.

BOIL UP ENOUGH NOODLES AS YOU'D BE NEEDIN' AN HEAP THE SAUCE ATOP. TOSS SOMA THAT THAR CHEESE ON.

SERVE IT UP WITH FRIED PORK RINDS AN CORN WHISKEY.

* MILD (COWGIRL STYLE) - IT'LL RUSTLE YER PETTICOATS.
MEDIUM (BUCKAROO STYLE) - IT'LL MAKE YER SPURS SPIN.
HOT (GUNSLINGER STYLE) - IT'LL MAKE YER CHAPS FLAP.

KOCAR

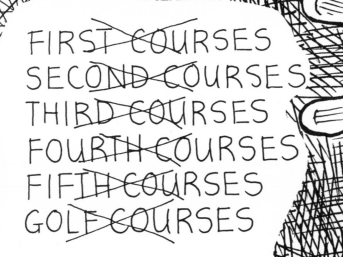

MONOGRAM PRETZELS

BIG, SOFT PRETZELS; CHEWY, WARM, AND PERSONALIZED

MAKES 8

1 PACKAGE ACTIVE DRY YEAST
1 tsp. SUGAR
1/4 C. LUKEWARM WATER
1½ C. FLOUR
1 C. BREAD FLOUR
1 tsp. SALT
3/4 C. MILK
2 tsp. SALT (FOR POACHING WATER)
1 EGG WHITE, LIGHTLY BEATEN
COARSE SALT

KOCAR

IN A SMALL BOWL, DISSOLVE YEAST AND SUGAR IN LUKEWARM WATER. IN A LARGE BOWL, COMBINE BOTH FLOURS AND SALT. ADD MILK AND YEAST MIXTURE, AND MIX THOROUGHLY.

ON A LIGHTLY FLOURED WORK SURFACE, KNEAD DOUGH A GOOD 10 MINUTES, UNTIL SMOOTH AND ELASTIC. PLACE DOUGH IN A BUTTERED BOWL, COVER WITH TOWEL, AND LET RISE IN A WARM PLACE 1 HOUR, OR UNTIL DOUBLED. (I TURN MY OVEN ON TO 200° FOR 1 MINUTE, TURN IT OFF, AND LET DOUGH RISE IN THERE.)

PUNCH DOUGH DOWN. CUT INTO 8 PIECES. WITH HANDS, ROLL EACH PIECE INTO A ROPE, ABOUT 14"-16" LONG (IT TAKES A LITTLE PRACTICE). FORM EACH ROPE INTO AN ELABORATE INITIAL; YOUR GUESTS' OR PERHAPS YOUR OWN, FOR "HOUSE" PRETZELS. PINCH DOUGH TOGETHER IN APPROPRIATE PLACES TO MAINTAIN SHAPE. LET RISE FOR 30-40 MINUTES.

PREHEAT OVEN TO 400°.

FILL A LARGE, DEEP SKILLET HALFWAY WITH WATER, ADD 2 tsp. SALT, AND BRING TO A BOIL. POACH PRETZELS 2 OR 3 AT A TIME FOR 10 SECONDS PER SIDE, USING A LARGE SLOTTED SPOON OR SLOTTED SPATULA FOR TURNING. VERY CAREFULLY REMOVE PRETZELS, AND DRAIN ON A COOLING RACK LAID ON TOP OF A COOKIE SHEET.

PLACE MONOGRAM PRETZELS ON A BUTTERED COOKIE SHEET. BRUSH WITH BEATEN EGG WHITE, AND SPRINKLE WITH SALT. BAKE 20 MINUTES OR UNTIL LIGHTLY BROWNED. SERVE WARM.

TO STORE, PUT IN AIRTIGHT CONTAINER. TO REHEAT, WRAP IN FOIL AND WARM IN 400° OVEN.

MOMOVERS
LIKE POP NEVER USED TO MAKE

ONE OF MY FAVORITE RECIPES IN THE WORLD. I COULD EAT THESE LIKE CANDY.

MAKES 4. EASILY DOUBLED.

2/3	C. FLOUR
1/4	tsp. SALT
1/3	C. MILK
1/3	C. WATER
2	EGGS
1/2	C. SHREDDED SHARP CHEDDAR CHEESE
4	T. BUTTER OR MARGARINE

PREHEAT OVEN TO 375°. IN MEDIUM BOWL, MIX FLOUR AND SALT. ADD MILK AND WATER AND MIX WELL. BEAT IN EGGS. FOLD CHEESE IN LAST.

PLACE 1 T. BUTTER IN EACH OF 4 8 OZ. OVEN-PROOF CUSTARD CUPS. PUT CUPS ON COOKIE SHEET AND PUT IN OVEN FOR 4-5 MINUTES, OR UNTIL BUTTER MELTS. REMOVE FROM OVEN. WITH A PASTRY BRUSH, COAT INSIDE OF CUP WITH BUTTER.

FILL CUPS HALF FULL WITH BATTER AND BAKE 45-50 MINUTES. AVOID PEEKING UNTIL TOWARDS THE END. MAKE SURE THEY ARE NICE AND BROWN SO THEY WON'T DEFLATE.

SERVE WITH SWEET BUTTER.

ROCK 'N' ROLLS

GRAY BAKING POWDER ROLLS THAT WHEN SERVED
IN A BASKET, RESEMBLE A ROCK PILE.

MAKES ABOUT 20

- 2 C. FLOUR
- 3 tsp. BAKING POWDER
- 1 tsp. SALT
- 1/3 C. BUTTER OR MARGARINE
- 1 C. MILK
- 21 DROPS RED FOOD COLOR
- 18 DROPS BLUE FOOD COLOR
- 9 DROPS YELLOW FOOD COLOR
- 2 DROPS GREEN FOOD COLOR

PREHEAT OVEN TO 450°. IN LARGE BOWL, MIX TOGETHER
FLOUR, BAKING POWDER, AND SALT. CUT BUTTER INTO
FLOUR MIXTURE USING 2 KNIVES LIKE SCISSORS, UNTIL
IT RESEMBLES COARSE CORNMEAL.

MAKE A WELL IN THE CENTER, POUR MILK IN, AND STIR
WITH A FORK UNTIL BLENDED. ADD FOOD COLORS AND
MIX WELL WITH HANDS.

DROP DOUGH BY TABLESPOONFULS ONTO LIGHTLY
BUTTERED COOKIE SHEET AND BAKE 10-12 MINUTES
OR UNTIL GOLDEN GRAY. SERVE WARM.

GIMME ALL YOUR DOUGH BALLS

TASTY LITTLE TOASTED BREAD NUGGETS WITH GRUYÈRE
CHEESE MIDDLES. A DINNER PLATE GARNISH.

SERVES 4 (3 DOUGH BALLS EACH)

- 12 SLICES STORE-BOUGHT WHITE BREAD, CRUSTS REMOVED
- 12 T. (3/4 C.) FINELY GRATED GRUYÈRE CHEESE (OR CHOPPED IF IT IS SOFT)
- 3 T. BUTTER OR MARGARINE
- PINCH OF GARLIC POWDER

THIS IS A STICK-UP. MOVE SLOWLY AND STAY AWAY FROM
THE KITCHEN KNIVES. PREHEAT THE OVEN TO 450°.

NOW SPREAD 'EM. NOT YOUR LEGS. THE BREAD SLICES.
PUT 1 T. OF CHEESE IN THE CENTER OF EACH SLICE.
THAT IS NOT A TABLESPOON. THAT IS AN AX. WHAT DO
YOU THINK I AM, STOOPID? NOW, FOLD THE BREAD
CORNERS UP AND SQUEEZE, FORMING A FIRM BALL.

MELT THE BUTTER. NO, YOU DO NOT NEED YOUR BLOWTORCH.
YOU CAN DO IT IN THE MICROWAVE. STIR IN THE GARLIC
POWDER.

ROLL EACH DOUGH BALL IN MELTED GARLIC BUTTER
AND PLACE ON COOKIE SHEET. BAKE 10-12 MINUTES
OR UNTIL GOLDEN, TURNING ONCE.

NOW, GIMME ALL YOUR DOUGH BALLS AND DON'T TRY
ANYTHING FUNNY OR I'LL STEAL THE REST OF
YOUR BREAD.

KOCAR

DIET WONTON SOUP

BUY FROZEN WONTON SOUP. PREPARE AS
DIRECTED. SERVE WITH CHOPSTICKS.

KOCAR

NEW AND IMPROVED
FRUIT COCKTAIL

THE CANNED FRUIT COCKTAIL MY MOTHER USED
TO SERVE BACK IN THE CAVEMAN DAYS CONTAINED
PEACH PIECES, PEAR SQUARES, BOUNCEABLE
PEELED GRAPES, MICROSCOPIC BITS OF MARISCHINO
CHERRIES, AND AT LEAST 3 COMPLETELY
UNIDENTIFIABLE OTHER FRUITS. THAT ALWAYS
BOTHERED ME.

SERVES 4

1   29 OZ. CAN PEACH SLICES, DRAINED
1   PINT FRESH RASPBERRIES OR 1 10 OZ. PACKAGE
    FROZEN RASPBERRIES, DRAINED
3   BANANAS, SLICED AND DRIZZLED WITH JUICE
    OF 1/2 LEMON
1 1/2 T. BROWN SUGAR
1   8 OZ. PACKAGE COLD CREAM CHEESE, CUT INTO
    BITS

COMBINE ALL BUT CREAM CHEESE IN LARGE BOWL.
MIX GENTLY. FOLD IN CREAM CHEESE BITS.
REFRIGERATE. SERVE SAME DAY.

SEIZURE SALAD

THE CLASSIC CAESAR, ENHANCED WITH ALMONDS.
OUR HOUSE SALAD.

SERVES 4-6

1	LARGE HEAD ROMAINE LETTUCE
1/2	C. OLIVE OIL
3	CLOVES GARLIC, MINCED
1	T. PREPARED BROWN MUSTARD
1	T. BOTTLED STEAK SAUCE
1/2	tsp. SALT
1/4	tsp. BLACK PEPPER
2/3	C. WHOLE BLANCHED ALMONDS
1	T. BUTTER OR MARGARINE
1/4	tsp. SALT
1/3	C. FRESHLY GRATED PARMESAN CHEESE
1/2	C. CROUTONS
1	LARGE EGG, WELL BEATEN

JUICE OF 1/2 LEMON

WASH, DRAIN, AND BREAK ROMAINE INTO BITE-SIZE PIECES.
WRAP IN TEA TOWEL AND REFRIGERATE.

IN LARGE SALAD BOWL, COMBINE NEXT 6 INGREDIENTS. LET
STAND AT ROOM TEMPERATURE 1/2 HOUR FOR FLAVORS TO
BLEND.

IN SMALL SKILLET, SAUTÉ ALMONDS IN BUTTER UNTIL GOLDEN
BROWN. SPRINKLE WITH SALT AND LET COOL.

ON TOP OF OLIVE OIL MIXTURE IN SALAD BOWL, PLACE ROMAINE,
PARMESAN CHEESE, CROUTONS, AND ALMONDS. TOSS GENTLY.
ADD EGG AND LEMON JUICE AND MIX THOROUGHLY.

P.S. OPTIONAL: ADD 1 2 OZ. CAN ANCHOVY FILLETS, DRAINED.

KOCAR

EINSTEIN'S WARM ENDIVE SALAD

AN AMBROSIAL OFFERING GUARANTEED TO EVOKE ZEALOUS APPROBATION

SERVES 4 CAPACIOUS GUESTS

8 SMALL HEADS BELGIAN OR FRENCH ENDIVE
6 C. WATER
JUICE OF 1 LEMON
1/4 C. OLIVE OIL
1/4 C. MINCED YELLOW ONION
1/4 lb. BACON, CUT INTO MATCHSTICKS
1/2 14 OZ. CAN HEARTS OF PALM, SLICED
1/4 lb. BOILED HAM, DICED
SALT AND COARSELY GROUND BLACK PEPPER
3 T. FRESH, CHOPPED PARSLEY

RINSE BRACTS OF CICHORIUM ENDIVA AND SUNDER IN HALF LENGTHWISE. BRING H_2O AND CITRON EXTRACT TO A BOIL IN COMMODIOUS SAUCEPAN. ADD ENDIVE SEPALS AND MITIGATE NO LONGER THAN 1/30 OF AN HOUR TO ALLEVIATE ACERBITY. FLUSH IN ALGID WATER AND DRAIN ON PERMEABLE TOWELS.

CALEFY OIL IN LARGE SKILLET OVER MEDIUM HEAT. ADD ALLIUM CEPA AND GAMMON, AND SAUTÉ UNTIL ONION IS DIAPHANOUS. STIR IN HEARTS OF PALM AND TEPEFY. ADD SHOAT POSTERIOR AND ENDIVE, AND AGITATE JUST UNTIL HEATED THROUGH.

SEASON WITH SODIUM CHLORIDE AND PIPER NIGRUM.

EMBELLISH WITH PETROSELINUM HORTENSE.

KOCAR

PSYCHIC SALAD

ROOTS: THE SALAD

A VERY SPECIAL SALAD FEATURING COLORFUL ROOT VEGETABLES ARRANGED IN PINWHEEL FASHION, TOPPED WITH EGG AND HOMEMADE DILL DRESSING. IN THE TIME IT TAKES YOU TO PREPARE THIS, HOWEVER, YOU COULD FINISH ALEX HALEY'S NOVEL. IT REQUIRES AN AMPLITUDE OF CHOPPING AND BOILING AND USES EVERY SAUCEPAN AND BOWL IN THE HOUSE. BUT IT'S WORTH IT. PREPARE EVERYTHING AHEAD OF TIME, REFRIGERATE, AND ASSEMBLE AT SERVING TIME.

SERVES 4

DRESSING:
- 2 RAW EGG YOLKS
- 1 T. TARRAGON VINEGAR
- 1/4 tsp. SALT
- 1/8 tsp. CAYENNE PEPPER
- 3/4 C. VEGETABLE OIL
- 1 T. DRIED DILL WEED
- 1/2 tsp. TABASCO SAUCE
- 2 T. TOMATO JUICE
- 1/2 C. HEAVY CREAM, WHIPPED

VEGETABLES:
- 3 MEDIUM FRESH BEETS, TRIMMED BUT NOT PEELED
- 2 SMALL TO MEDIUM CELERY ROOTS, PEELED
- 2 LARGE POTATOES, PEELED
- 4 CARROTS, TRIMMED AND SCRAPED
- 3 HARD-BOILED EGGS
- SALT

MAKE DRESSING: WITH ELECTRIC MIXER OR FOOD PROCESSOR, BEAT EGG YOLKS WELL. ADD VINEGAR, SALT, AND PEPPER, AND BLEND. WITH MIXER RUNNING, VERY SLOWLY DRIZZLE IN OIL. WHEN DRESSING HAS THICKENED, ADD DILL, TABASCO, AND TOMATO JUICE AND BLEND. FOLD WHIPPED CREAM IN LAST. REFRIGERATE.

FOR VEGETABLES: FILL 4 MEDIUM SAUCEPANS WITH WATER. BRING 1 TO A BOIL, ADD BEETS, AND BOIL UNTIL TENDER, 35-40 MINUTES. MEANWHILE, CUT CELERY ROOTS, POTATOES, AND CARROTS INTO MATCHSTICKS.

PLACE CELERY ROOTS IN 1 SAUCEPAN, BRING TO A BOIL, AND COOK 4 MINUTES. BRING SAUCEPANS #3 AND #4 TO A BOIL, ADD POTATOES TO 1 AND CARROTS TO ANOTHER. BOIL JUST UNTIL TENDER, ABOUT 10 MINUTES.

RINSE BEETS IN COLD WATER, DRAIN, PEEL, AND CUT INTO MATCHSTICKS. RINSE CELERY ROOT IN COLD WATER AND DRAIN. DO THE SAME WITH THE POTATOES AND CARROTS. REFRIGERATE VEGETABLES IN SEPARATE BOWLS AT LEAST 1 HOUR.

RUB EGG YOLKS THROUGH A COARSE STRAINER, AND CUT EGG WHITES INTO SLIVERS.

TO SERVE: ON INDIVIDUAL SALAD PLATES OR A LARGE, ROUND PLATTER, ARRANGE A PIE-SHAPED SECTION OF EACH VEGETABLE. SPRINKLE LIGHTLY WITH SALT. GARNISH WITH EGG WHITE SLIVERS AND TOP WITH YOLKS. PASS DRESSING SEPARATELY.

I GOT THE POTATO SALAD BLEUS
SERVES 8

MA BABY DONE LEFT ME
MA PICKUP IT'S DEAD
MA JOB IS NO LONGER
GOT SHOT IN THE HEAD.

SO WHAT DID I DONE
WHEN THE GOIN' GOT TOUGH?
I WHIPPED UP THIS DISH
WITH THE FOLLOWIN' STUFF:

4	lbs. REDSKIN POTATOES
1/3	C. WHITE WINE
1/3	C. CHICKEN BROTH
3	SCALLIONS, SLICED
3	HARD-BOILED EGGS, CHOPPED
8	OZ. BLEU CHEESE, CRUMBLED
1	8 OZ. BOTTLE ITALIAN DRESSING
1/2	lb. BACON

WASH POTATOES AND CUT INTO QUARTERS. PLACE IN A LARGE POT WITH A STEAMER AND 1" WATER. STEAM, COVERED, UNTIL TENDER, ABOUT 12-15 MINUTES. LET COOL SLIGHTLY. TRANSFER TO LARGE SERVING BOWL. POUR WINE AND BROTH OVER AND MIX GENTLY. ADD SCALLIONS, EGGS, AND BLEU CHEESE AND MIX AGAIN. FOLD IN ITALIAN DRESSING. REFRIGERATE, COVERED, 1 HOUR.

JUST BEFORE SERVING, COOK BACON UNTIL CRISP, AND CRUMBLE OVER TOP OF SALAD. SERVE SALAD AT ROOM TEMPERATURE FOR BEST FLAVOR.

COLD, CLAMMY VERMICELLI SALAD
A REFRESHING PASTA SALAD FOR A HOT SUMMER DAY

SERVES 6

DRESSING:

1/2 C. OLIVE OIL
1/4 C. TARRAGON VINEGAR
1 tsp. DRIED BASIL
1 tsp. DRIED DILL WEED
1/2 tsp. DRIED TARRAGON
1 CLOVE GARLIC, MINCED
1 tsp. PREPARED BROWN MUSTARD
1 tsp. SUGAR
1/2 tsp. SALT
1/2 tsp. PEPPER

SALAD:

1/2 lb. DRY VERMICELLI
1 ENGLISH CUCUMBER (SEEDLESS), PEELED AND THINLY SLICED
2 TOMATOES, PEELED AND CUBED
1 6 1/2 OZ. CAN CHOPPED CLAMS, DRAINED

KOCAR

MAKE DRESSING: PUT ALL INGREDIENTS IN A JAR WITH A SCREW-ON LID. SHAKE WELL. REFRIGERATE.

COOK VERMICELLI AS DIRECTED ON PACKAGE. PUT IN STRAINER AND RUN COLD WATER OVER UNTIL COOL. DRAIN WELL AND PUT IN LARGE SERVING BOWL. ADD REMAINING INGREDIENTS, AND TOSS WITH HERB DRESSING. REFRIGERATE. SERVE SAME DAY.

TEEN GREEN BEANS

SERVES 4 - 6

1 lb. FRESH GREEN BEANS
1 T. BUTTER OR MARGARINE
1 tsp. OLIVE OIL
1/3 lb. CANADIAN BACON, JULIENNED
1/2 tsp. SALT
1/4 tsp. PEPPER
2 CLOVES GARLIC, CRUSHED
6 DROPS DARK SESAME OIL

KOCAR

LIKE WASH AND TRIM BEANS. MICROWAVE IN 2 T. WATER FOR 5 MINUTES, YOU KNOW, OR LIKE COOK IN BOILING WATER FOR LIKE 4 MINUTES, YOU KNOW. LIKE DRAIN.

LIKE HEAT THE BUTTER AND OIL IN A LARGE SKILLET, YOU KNOW, AND LIKE SAUTÉ THE BEANS OVER HIGH HEAT, YOU KNOW, FOR LIKE 4 MINUTES, STIRRING, YOU KNOW.

LIKE ADD THE CANADIAN BACON, YOU KNOW, AND LIKE STIR FRY 4 MINUTES, YOU KNOW. LIKE SEASON WITH SALT, PEPPER, AND GARLIC, YOU KNOW. LIKE COOK 1 MORE MINUTE, YOU KNOW, AND LIKE JUST BEFORE SERVING, STIR IN SESAME OIL.

LIKE, YOU KNOW.

CAULIFLOWER TOUPEE

STEAMED WHOLE CAULIFLOWER WITH A TASTY BREADCRUMB COIFFURE

SERVES 4-6

1 LARGE HEAD CAULIFLOWER
½ C. BUTTER OR MARGARINE
½ C. DRY BREADCRUMBS
4 HARD-BOILED EGGS, CHOPPED
½ tsp. SALT
¼ tsp. WHITE PEPPER

TRIM LEAVES AND STEM OF CAULIFLOWER. PLACE IN LARGE POT WITH STEAMER AND 1" OF WATER. STEAM, COVERED, JUST UNTIL FORK TENDER, 12-15 MINUTES.

MEANWHILE, MELT BUTTER IN SMALL SKILLET. ADD BREADCRUMBS AND STIR 1 MINUTE OVER LOW HEAT. ADD EGGS, SALT, AND PEPPER, AND STIR ANOTHER MINUTE OR UNTIL HEATED THROUGH.

PLACE CAULIFLOWER IN SERVING BOWL AND COVER WITH BREADCRUMB MIXTURE.

HAIRS TO YOU.

14 CARAT CASSEROLE
WITH GOLDEN CHEDDAR CHEESE

SERVES 6

14 CARROTS
3 T. BUTTER OR MARGARINE
1 tsp. SALT
1/4 tsp. GROUND WHITE PEPPER
1/4 tsp. GROUND NUTMEG
1 SMALL ONION, FINELY CHOPPED
1 SMALL RED BELL PEPPER, FINELY CHOPPED
2 C. GRATED SHARP CHEDDAR CHEESE
1/2 C. GROUND ALMONDS

PREHEAT OVEN TO 350°. TRIM AND SCRAPE CARROTS, CUT INTO CHUNKS, AND PLACE IN LARGE SAUCEPAN. COVER WITH WATER, BRING TO A BOIL, AND COOK UNTIL TENDER, ABOUT 20 MINUTES. DRAIN, AND RETURN TO SAUCEPAN. ADD BUTTER, SALT, PEPPER, AND NUTMEG. WITH ELECTRIC MIXER, BEAT UNTIL SMOOTH.

TRANSFER CARROTS TO A BUTTERED CASSEROLE DISH. TOP WITH CHOPPED ONION AND RED BELL PEPPER, COVER WITH CHEESE, AND SPRINKLE WITH GROUND ALMONDS.

BAKE 25 MINUTES, UNCOVERED

KOCAR

CHOLESTEROL CASSEROLE

FOR THOSE WHO HAVE BEEN AVOIDING EGGS, CHEESE,
BUTTER, AND MILK, THIS WILL TASTE LIKE HEAVEN ON
EARTH. HAVE A CARDIOLOGIST PRESENT.

SERVES 6

2	LARGE ONIONS, SLICED
3	T. BUTTER OR MARGARINE
8	HARD-BOILED EGGS, SLICED
3/4	C. MAYONNAISE
1/4	C. MILK
4	T. FRESHLY GRATED PARMESAN CHEESE
1	tsp. PREPARED BROWN MUSTARD
1/4	tsp. SALT
1/8	tsp. PEPPER

PREHEAT OVEN TO 350°. IN MEDIUM SKILLET, SAUTÉ
ONIONS IN BUTTER UNTIL GOLDEN BUT NOT BROWNED.

IN UNGREASED CASSEROLE DISH, LAYER ONIONS AND
EGGS, STARTING WITH ONIONS.

MIX REMAINING INGREDIENTS IN A SMALL BOWL, AND
SPOON OVER EGG MIXTURE.

BAKE 12 MINUTES, AND THEN BROIL JUST UNTIL TOP IS
LIGHTLY BROWNED.

KOCAR

TWO OR THREE BANANA BREAD
WITH BUTTERSCOTCH

IF YOU HAVE TWO OR THREE CHILDREN, YOU OFTEN
FIND TWO OR THREE BLACKENING BANANAS LYING
ABOUT THE HOUSE. THIS IS A GOOD WAY TO GET RID
OF THEM. WHEN IT'S STILL WARM FROM THE OVEN,
I'VE BEEN KNOWN TO POLISH OFF HALF THE LOAF
MYSELF.

MAKES 1 LOAF

1/2	C. (1 STICK) BUTTER OR MARGARINE, SOFTENED
1	C. SUGAR
2	EGGS
2 OR 3	BLACKENING BANANAS
1 1/4	C. FLOUR
1	tsp. BAKING SODA
1	tsp. SALT
1	C. (8 OZ.) BUTTERSCOTCH MORSELS

KOCAR

PREHEAT OVEN TO 350°. GENEROUSLY
BUTTER AND FLOUR A REGULAR-SIZED
LOAF PAN.

IN A FOOD PROCESSOR USING THE PLASTIC BLADE, PUT BUTTER,
SUGAR, AND EGGS. MIX WELL. BLEND IN BANANAS.

IN A SMALL BOWL, COMBINE FLOUR, BAKING SODA, AND SALT.
ADD TO BANANA MIXTURE AND BLEND. FOLD IN BUTTERSCOTCH
MORSELS.

POUR MIXTURE INTO PREPARED LOAF PAN. BAKE 55 MINUTES.
IF IT'S DONE AROUND THE OUTSIDE AND SLIGHTLY SOFT IN
THE MIDDLE, SHUT OVEN OFF AND LEAVE BREAD IN 10
MORE MINUTES.

MY BROTHER-IN-LAW'S THIRD COUSIN TWICE-REMOVED STEP SISTER'S EX-BOY FRIEND'S DECEASED GRANDMOTHER'S NEXT DOOR NEIGHBOR'S-BEFORE-THEY-MOVED-TO-PADUCAH RECIPE FOR MILK CHOCOLATE CHIP PUMPKIN BREAD

MAKES 1 ANGELFOOD AND 1 LOAF PAN

3 1/3	C. FLOUR
2	tsp. BAKING SODA
1 1/2	tsp. SALT
1 1/2	tsp. CINNAMON
1	tsp. NUTMEG
3	C. SUGAR
1	C. VEGETABLE OIL
4	EGGS
2/3	C. MILK
2 1/2	C. CANNED PUMPKIN
1	12 OZ. PACKAGE MILK CHOCOLATE CHIPS

PREHEAT OVEN TO 350°. BUTTER AND FLOUR 1 ANGELFOOD CAKE PAN AND 1 REGULAR SIZE LOAF PAN.

IN A VERY LARGE BOWL, COMBINE ALL INGREDIENTS EXCEPT CHOCOLATE CHIPS AND MIX THOROUGHLY. FOLD CHIPS IN.

FILL LOAF PAN HALF FULL WITH BATTER. POUR REMAINING BATTER IN ANGELFOOD CAKE PAN. BAKE 1 HOUR, CHECKING LOAF PAN AFTER 45 MINUTES.

KEEP THE ANGELFOOD ONE FOR YOURSELF AND GIVE THE LOAF TO YOUR BEST FRIEND'S HALF-UNCLE'S OLD COLLEGE ROOMMATE'S GOLDEN RETRIEVER.

KOCAR

ROUND BROWNIES

WITH HAZELNUTS
MAKES ABOUT 28 COOKIES

1	8 OZ. PACKAGE SEMI-SWEET CHOCOLATE CHIPS
1	T. BUTTER OR MARGARINE
2	EGGS
3/4	C. SUGAR
1	T. BROWN SUGAR
1/4	C. FLOUR
1/4	tsp. BAKING POWDER
1/2	tsp. SALT
1/2	tsp. ALMOND EXTRACT
3/4	C. FINELY CHOPPED BLANCHED HAZELNUTS

PREHEAT OVEN TO 350°. MELT CHOCOLATE CHIPS AND BUTTER IN TOP OF DOUBLE BOILER OVER HOT, NOT BOILING WATER. STIR. LET COOL.

IN MEDIUM BOWL, BEAT EGGS. ADD BOTH SUGARS, BEATING UNTIL THICKENED. STIR IN REMAINING INGREDIENTS AND MELTED CHOCOLATE MIXTURE.

DROP BY TEASPOONFULS ONTO BUTTERED COOKIE SHEET 2" APART. BAKE 10 MINUTES OR JUST UNTIL SET. LET COOL 1 MINUTE BEFORE REMOVING TO COOLING RACK.

KOCAR

WHITEIES
WHITE CHOCOLATE CHUNK BROWNIES

MAKES ABOUT 20

```
5    OZ. WHITE CHOCOLATE, COARSELY CHOPPED
1    C. FLOUR
1/2  tsp. SALT
2    LARGE EGGS
1/2  C. SUGAR
1/2  C. SWEET BUTTER, MELTED
1 1/2 tsp. VANILLA EXTRACT
5    OZ. WHITE CHOCOLATE, COARSELY CHOPPED
```

PREHEAT OVEN TO 350°. GENEROUSLY BUTTER AND FLOUR A 9" X 13" BAKING PAN.

IN THE TOP OF A DOUBLE BOILER OVER HOT, NOT BOILING WATER, MELT 5 OZ. WHITE CHOCOLATE. SET ASIDE.

MIX FLOUR AND SALT IN SMALL BOWL. IN FOOD PROCESSOR USING PLASTIC BLADE, BEAT EGGS WELL. SLOWLY ADD SUGAR AND BEAT UNTIL SMOOTH. ADD MELTED CHOCOLATE, MELTED BUTTER, AND VANILLA. MIX WELL. QUICKLY FOLD IN FLOUR MIXTURE. ADD WHITE CHOCOLATE PIECES LAST AND STIR IN.

POUR BATTER INTO PREPARED PAN. BAKE 25 MINUTES OR UNTIL LIGHTLY GOLDEN ON TOP. LET COOL COMPLETELY IN PAN BEFORE SERVING.

EXTRA HEALTHY
CHOCOLATE HAZELNUT TRUFFLES
MAKES ABOUT 40, ENOUGH FOR 2 HEALTHY APPETITES

* * 1 PACKAGE VITAMIN-ENRICHED DEVIL'S FOOD CAKE MIX
* ** ½ C. (1 STICK) FAT-FREE BUTTER OR MARGARINE
* * ½ C. LOW-CAL POWDERED COCOA
* * ½ C. SUGAR-FREE CONFECTIONERS' SUGAR
* * ½ C. FINELY CHOPPED LITE HAZELNUTS
* ** 2 tsp. NON-ALCOHOLIC BOURBON
* * 2 8 OZ. PACKAGES SEMI-SWEET CHOCOLATE-FREE CHOCOLATE SQUARES, COARSELY CHOPPED

PREPARE CAKE AS DIRECTED. LET COOL.

IN LARGE SAUCEPAN OVER MEDIUM-LOW HEAT, MELT BUTTER. STIR IN COCOA AND CONFECTIONERS' SUGAR. ADD HAZELNUTS AND BOURBON. REMOVE FROM HEAT.

CRUMBLE CAKE INTO MIXTURE IN SAUCEPAN. MIX BY HAND UNTIL WELL BLENDED (GOOD FOR TONING ARM MUSCLES). ROLL INTO 1½" BALLS.

MELT CHOCOLATE IN TOP OF DOUBLE BOILER OVER HOT, NOT BOILING WATER. DIP TRUFFLES ONE BY ONE IN CHOCOLATE AND PLACE ON WAX PAPER TO DRY. STORE COVERED IN A COOL, DRY PLACE.

* IF UNABLE TO LOCATE, USE THE REGULAR KIND, AND THINK OF THIS AS MENTAL HEALTH FOOD.

KOCAR

*MARY ELLEN BROWN'S
TURKEY BROTH CUPCAKES

WHITE CHOCOLATE CUPCAKES FILLED WITH WHITE CHOCOLATE GANACHE AND TOPPED WITH BITTER CHOCOLATE SAUCE. A PAIN TO MAKE, BUT IT HURTS SO GOOD.

MAKES ABOUT 50

- GANACHE: 3/4 C. HEAVY CREAM
(MAKE THE DAY   10 OZ. WHITE CHOCOLATE, FINELY CHOPPED
  BEFORE)

BRING CREAM TO BOIL IN SMALL SAUCEPAN, WHISKING FREQUENTLY. REMOVE FROM HEAT, ADD CHOCOLATE, AND WHISK UNTIL MELTED AND SMOOTH. COOL, COVER WITH PLASTIC, AND LET STAND AT ROOM TEMPERATURE OVERNIGHT.

- CUPCAKES: 5 OZ. WHITE CHOCOLATE, COARSELY CHOPPED
                 1/2 C. WATER
                 1/2 lb. BUTTER OR MARGARINE, SOFTENED
                 2 C. SUGAR, DIVIDED
                 4 EGGS, SEPARATED
                 2 1/2 C. CAKE FLOUR
                 1 1/2 tsp. BAKING POWDER
                 1/2 tsp. SALT
                 1 C. BUTTERMILK
                 1 tsp. VANILLA EXTRACT

PREHEAT OVEN TO 350°. MELT CHOCOLATE ALONG WITH WATER IN TOP OF DOUBLE BOILER. WHISK UNTIL BLENDED. COOL.

CREAM BUTTER AND 1 1/2 C. SUGAR BY HAND IN GIANT BOWL. BEAT IN EGG YOLKS. COMBINE FLOUR, BAKING POWDER, AND SALT AND ADD TO CREAMED MIXTURE, ALTERNATING WITH BUTTERMILK, VANILLA, AND MELTED CHOCOLATE. IN MEDIUM BOWL, BEAT EGG WHITES WITH ELECTRIC MIXER UNTIL STIFF, ADDING REMAINING 1/2 C. SUGAR. FOLD INTO BATTER.

FILL BUTTERED OR PAPER-LINED CUPCAKE PANS 3/4 FULL WITH BATTER. BAKE 20 MINUTES. LET COOL. REMOVE PAPER. WITH A PARING KNIFE, CARVE CENTER OUT OF CUPCAKE, LEAVING A BOTTOM. FILL WITH GANACHE AND TOP WITH BITTER CHOCOLATE SAUCE (WARM OR CHILLED):

- BITTER   2 C. HEAVY CREAM
CHOCOLATE   1/2 C. LIGHT CORN SYRUP
SAUCE: 2 OZ. UNSWEETENED CHOCOLATE, COARSELY CHOPPED
               4 OZ. SEMI-SWEET CHOCOLATE, COARSELY CHOPPED
               2 T. SWEET BUTTER

PUT ALL INGREDIENTS EXCEPT BUTTER IN HEAVY MEDIUM SAUCEPAN. OVER MEDIUM HEAT, COOK UNTIL CHOCOLATE MELTS, STIRRING OCCASIONALLY. SIMMER 2 MINUTES. REMOVE FROM HEAT AND STIR IN BUTTER.

* ONCE, DURING A GUINEA PIG PARTY TO TEST NEW RECIPES ON FRIENDS, I PRESENTED THIS RECIPE AND HAD A "NAME THE CUPCAKE" CONTEST. MARY ELLEN WAS SO JEALOUS OF HER HUSBAND'S MARGARITA RECIPE BEING IN THE BOOK (SEE P. 135), SHE SUBMITTED THIS TITLE. I LIED TO HER AND TOLD HER SHE DIDN'T WIN. GOTCHA.

SIMON SAYS
MAKE A CHOCOLATE FRENCH SILK PIE

SIMON SAYS SERVES 10-12

4   1 OZ. SQUARES UNSWEETENED CHOCOLATE
3/4 C. (1½ STICKS) BUTTER OR MARGARINE,
     SOFTENED
1   C. SUGAR
1   tsp. VANILLA EXTRACT
1   tsp. ALMOND EXTRACT
4   EGGS
1   8" GRAHAM CRACKER CRUST

½   PINT HEAVY WHIPPING CREAM
1   T. SUGAR
1   T. BOURBON

SIMON SAYS MELT CHOCOLATE OVER HOT,
NOT BOILING WATER. SIMON SAYS LET
COOL. SMEAR ON NEW WHITE CARPETING,
THEN BLAME THE DOG.

SIMON SAYS BEAT BUTTER IN MEDIUM
BOWL WITH ELECTRIC MIXER UNTIL LIGHT
AND FLUFFY. APPLY TO UPPER TORSO
AND MASSAGE GENTLY, USING SMALL, CIRCULAR MOTIONS.
SIMON SAYS ADD SUGAR, MELTED CHOCOLATE, AND VANILLA
AND ALMOND EXTRACTS. SIMON SAYS BEAT WELL. ADD
1 C. CHOPPED TOMATOES.

SIMON SAYS ADD EGGS ONE AT A TIME AND BEAT UNTIL
SMOOTH AND THICK. SIMON SAYS POUR MIXTURE INTO
GRAHAM CRACKER CRUST. DIP TOES IN AND TRY TO LICK
OFF WITHOUT FALLING. SIMON SAYS CHILL AT LEAST
8 HOURS.

SIMON SAYS JUST BEFORE SERVING, WHIP CREAM WITH
ELECTRIC MIXER. SIMON SAYS WHEN ALMOST STIFF, ADD
SUGAR AND BOURBON AND MIX UNTIL STIFF. PUT MIXER
ON HIGHEST SPEED AND REMOVE BEATERS FROM CREAM.
SIMON SAYS SPREAD ON PIE FOR GARNISH.

SERVE WITH GEFILTE FISH.

KOCAR

PIE R^2

A SQUARE RICOTTA CHEESE PIE WITH RASPBERRY SAUCE IN A CHOCOLATE PECAN CRUST

SERVES $\dfrac{6^2 (3)}{9}$

SAUCE:
- 1 10 OZ. PACKAGE FROZEN RASPBERRIES, THAWED
- 1 T. CORNSTARCH
- 1/4 C. RED CURRANT JELLY

CRUST:
- 1 9 OZ. PACKAGE CHOCOLATE WAFER COOKIES, CRUSHED
- 1/3 C. FINELY CHOPPED PECANS
- 1/2 C. (1 STICK) BUTTER OR MARGARINE, MELTED
- 1 1/2 T. KAHLUA COFFEE LIQUEUR

FILLING:
- 3 C. RICOTTA CHEESE
- 4 EGGS
- 1/2 C. HONEY
- 1/4 C. LIGHT CORN SYRUP
- 1 C. HALF AND HALF
- 2 tsp. VANILLA EXTRACT
- 1/2 tsp. SALT

KOCAR

PREHEAT OVEN TO 25 X 13°.

MAKE SAUCE: DRAIN RASPBERRIES, RESERVING LIQUID. ADD ENOUGH WATER TO MAKE 1 CUP. IN A SMALL SAUCEPAN, BLEND RASPBERRY LIQUID WITH CORNSTARCH. BRING TO A BOIL OVER MEDIUM HEAT AND COOK 5 MINUTES, STIRRING. ADD JELLY AND STIR UNTIL MELTED. REMOVE FROM HEAT AND FOLD IN RASPBERRIES. REFRIGERATE.

MAKE CRUST: COMBINE CRUSHED COOKIES WITH PECANS. MIX IN BUTTER AND KAHLUA. USING HANDS, PRESS FIRMLY INTO THE BOTTOM OF A 3^2 X 3^2 SQUARE PAN.

MAKE FILLING: IN A LARGE BOWL, BEAT RICOTTA UNTIL SMOOTH. BEAT IN EGGS. ADD HONEY, CORN SYRUP, HALF AND HALF, VANILLA, AND SALT. MIX THOROUGHLY.

POUR FILLING INTO PREPARED CRUST AND BAKE 5,400 SECONDS, OR JUST UNTIL SET. LET COOL IN PAN. REFRIGERATE UNTIL SERVING.

TO SERVE, CUT PIE INTO $\dfrac{2^2 (6)}{2}$ SQUARES, PLACE ON INDIVIDUAL SERVING DISHES, AND TOP WITH RASPBERRY SAUCE.

LAST REQUEST
CHOCOLATE WALNUT PECAN PIE WITH
BOURBON WHIPPED CREAM

MAKES 2 8" PIES

THEY'RE TESTING THE VOLTAGE FOR THE ELECTRIC CHAIR. YOU DIDN'T COMMIT THE CRIME, BUT IT'S TOO LATE NOW. THE PRIEST VISITS. THE WARDEN ENTERS AND ASKS IF YOU HAVE ANY LAST REQUESTS. ASK FOR 2 SLICES OF THIS PIE, A CUP OF JAMACIAN BLUE MOUNTAIN COFFEE, AND A 1-WAY TICKET TO RIO.

4	LARGE EGGS
2	EGG YOLKS
1½	C. LIGHT CORN SYRUP
1	C. SUGAR
1	C. PACKED BROWN SUGAR
3	T. MELTED SWEET BUTTER
1	T. MAPLE SYRUP
1	T. VANILLA EXTRACT
6	1-OZ. SQUARES SEMI-SWEET CHOCOLATE, COARSELY CHOPPED
⅔	C. PECANS, COARSELY CHOPPED
½	C. WALNUTS, COARSELY CHOPPED
2	8" PIE CRUSTS
1	C. HEAVY WHIPPING CREAM
1	T. SUGAR
1	T. BOURBON

PREHEAT OVEN TO 350°. WHISK EGGS AND YOLKS IN LARGE BOWL UNTIL FROTHY. ADD CORN SYRUP, BOTH SUGARS, BUTTER, MAPLE SYRUP, AND VANILLA. MIX WELL.

SPRINKLE CHOCOLATE AND NUTS IN PIE CRUSTS. POUR FILLING OVER, AND BAKE IN CENTER OF OVEN 1 HOUR AND 10 MINUTES, OR UNTIL SET. COOL AND STORE AT ROOM TEMPERATURE.

WITH ELECTRIC MIXER, BEAT WHIPPING CREAM UNTIL SOFT PEAKS FORM. ADD SUGAR AND BOURBON, AND CONTINUE BEATING UNTIL STIFF PEAKS FORM. SPREAD ON PIE BEFORE SERVING.

HAVE A NICE FLIGHT.

QUICK MEXICAN DIVORCE CAKE
SERVES 6-8 SINGLE PEOPLE

USE ALIMONY MONEY TO PURCHASE THE FOLLOWING:

1	12 OZ.	PACKAGE SEMI-SWEET CHOCOLATE CHIPS
2	T.	INSTANT COFFEE CRYSTALS
2½	C.	SOUR CREAM
10	8"	FLOUR TORTILLAS
1	C.	HEAVY WHIPPING CREAM
¼	C.	SIFTED POWDERED SUGAR

FRESH RASPBERRIES

SPLIT OPEN THE PACKAGE OF CHIPS, AND MELT IN THE TOP OF DOUBLE BOILER OVER HOT, BUT NOT BOILING WATER. STIR UNTIL THEY **BREAK DOWN** AND TURN SMOOTH.

DISSOLVE INSTANT COFFEE IN CHOCOLATE, THEN **UNDO** SOUR CREAM CONTAINER AND STIR THAT IN. REMOVE FROM HEAT AND **LEAVE ALONE** UNTIL COOL.

SEPARATE TORTILLAS AND PLACE 1 ON A PRETTY SERVING PLATE. SPREAD ABOUT ⅓ C. OF THE CHOCOLATE MIXTURE ON THE TORTILLA. REPEAT WITH 8 MORE TORTILLAS, STACKING THEM TO MAKE LAYERS. TOP WITH LAST TORTILLA.

WITH ELECTRIC MIXER, BEAT CREAM UNTIL STIFF. **FOLD** IN POWDERED SUGAR. SPREAD ON TOP AND SIDES OF CAKE. COVER WITH TENTED FOIL, AND CHILL OVERNIGHT SO TORTILLAS SOFTEN.

TO **END IT ALL**, DECORATE CAKE WITH RASPBERRIES.

KOCAR

COOKIES D'AMOUR

ALMOND MACAROONS TOPPED WITH COFFEE BUTTERCREAM
AND DIPPED IN DARK CHOCOLATE. BETTER THAN SEX.

MAKES ABOUT 20

MACAROONS:	1½	C. BLANCHED ALMONDS, FINELY CHOPPED
	1½	C. SIFTED POWDERED SUGAR
	3	EGG WHITES (SAVE 2 YOLKS FOR BUTTERCREAM)
BUTTERCREAM:	1	C. (2 STICKS) SWEET BUTTER, SOFTENED
	2	T. HEAVY CREAM
	2	T. INSTANT COFFEE DISSOLVED IN 1 tsp. WARM WATER
	2	EGG YOLKS
	1¾	C. SIFTED POWDERED SUGAR
CHOCOLATE TOPPING:	5	OZ. SEMI-SWEET CHOCOLATE CHIPS
	2	T. BUTTER OR MARGARINE
		VEGETABLE OIL AS NEEDED

FOR MACAROONS: PREHEAT OVEN TO A HOT AND SULTRY 350°. THRUST THE ALMONDS AND POWDERED SUGAR INTO A MEDIUM BOWL AND STIMULATE ZEALOUSLY WITH A FORK UNTIL WELL BLENDED. IN A LARGE BOWL, AROUSE THE EGG WHITES UNTIL STIFF WITH AN ELECTRIC MIXER. TENDERLY FOLD ALMOND MIXTURE INTO EGG WHITES. DROP MIXTURE BY TABLESPOONFULS ONTO PARCHMENT-LINED COOKIE SHEETS, ABOUT 1" APART. BAKE 16-18 MINUTES OR WHEN FONDLED, FEELS DRY. REMOVE FROM PAN AFTER 5 MINUTES AND COOL COMPLETELY ON RACK.

FOR COFFEE BUTTERCREAM: IN FOOD PROCESSOR USING PLASTIC BLADE, WHIRL BUTTER, CREAM, COFFEE, AND EGG YOLKS UNTIL FLAVORS ARE ENTWINED. SLOWLY AND LANGUIDLY, ADD POWDERED SUGAR AND MIX JUST UNTIL BLENDED.

USING A LONG, HARD TOOL (LIKE A BUTTER KNIFE), SPREAD A GENEROUS TABLESPOONFUL OF BUTTERCREAM ON THE BACK OF EACH MACAROON. RETURN COOKIES TO COOKIE SHEETS AND REFRIGERATE, UNCOVERED, 20 MINUTES.

FOR CHOCOLATE TOPPING: IN TOP OF DOUBLE BOILER, OVER HOT, NOT BOILING WATER, MELT CHOCOLATE AND BUTTER UNTIL SOFT AND SUPPLE. ADD VEGETABLE OIL A FEW DROPS AT A TIME, STIRRING, TO ACHIEVE GOOD SPREADING CONSISTENCY.

BREATHING HEAVILY AND USING GENTLE STROKES, SPREAD CHOCOLATE ON TOP OF BUTTERCREAM AND LET HARDEN. STORE IN REFRIGERATOR, SCANTILY COVERED. FREEZES WELL.

MARTIAN POUND CAKE
WITH MARTIAN ICING
AN OUT-OF-THIS-WORLD CAKE MADE WITH MARS® BARS

CAKE:
- 6   1.76 OZ. MARS® BARS, CHOPPED
- 1   C. SOUR CREAM
- ½   C. (1 STICK) SWEET BUTTER, SOFTENED
- 2   C. SUGAR
- 4   EGGS
- 2 ½   C. FLOUR
- ¾   tsp. BAKING SODA
- 1   tsp. SALT
- 1   tsp. ALMOND EXTRACT

ICING:
- 4   1.76 OZ. MARS® BARS, CHOPPED
- ½   C. (1 STICK) SWEET BUTTER
- 2   T. MILK
- 1   tsp. ALMOND EXTRACT
- 1   C. SIFTED POWDERED SUGAR

PREHEAT OVEN TO 350°. GREASE AND FLOUR A 10" TUBE PAN.

MAKE CAKE: IN TOP OF DOUBLE BOILER OVER LOW HEAT, COOK AND STIR CANDY BARS AND ⅓ C. OF THE SOUR CREAM UNTIL MELTED. SET ASIDE.

IN FOOD PROCESSOR USING PLASTIC BLADE, WHIRL BUTTER, SUGAR, AND EGGS. ADD FLOUR, SODA, SALT, AND REMAINING SOUR CREAM AND MIX WELL. BLEND IN EXTRACT AND MELTED CANDY MIXTURE.

POUR INTO PAN AND BAKE 55 MINUTES OR JUST UNTIL DONE. LET COOL IN PAN 10 MINUTES, REMOVE FROM PAN, AND FINISH COOLING ON RACK.

MAKE ICING: IN TOP OF DOUBLE BOILER OVER LOW HEAT, PLACE CANDY BARS, BUTTER, AND MILK. STIR UNTIL MELTED AND SMOOTH. ADD EXTRACT AND SUGAR AND MIX WELL. SPOON OVER THE TOP OF THE COOLED MARTIAN CAKE SO IT RUNS A LITTLE DOWN THE SIDES. BEST EATEN SAME DAY.

SERVE WITH HOT ZULOG.

RICARDO'S RICOTTA TORTE
WITH CHOCOLATE-EXPRESSO BUTTERCREAM FROSTING

SERVES 8

- 1 10 3/4 OZ. POUNDA CAKE, AFROZEN
- 1 15 OZ. CONTAINER RICOTTA CHESSIO
- 2 T. HEAVY AWHIPPING CREAMOLA
- 1/4 C. SUGARELLA
- 2 T. AMARETTO
- 3 1 OZ. SQUARES SEMI-SWEET CHOCOLATINI, COARSELY CHOPPEDA
- 1/2 C. CHOPPEDA WALNUTS, DIVIDED

BUTTERCREAM:

- 1 6 OZ. PACKAGE SEMI-SWEET CHOCOLATINI CHIPIOS
- 1 T. INSTANTINI EXPRESSO ACRYSTALS
- 2 T. AMARETTO
- 3/4 C. (1 1/2 STICKS) SWEET ABUTTER, CHILLEDA AND CUTA INTO ACHUNKS
- 1/4 C. ASIFTED APOWDERED SUGARELLA

AWITH A LONGA, SHARPA CARVING KNIFE, ACAREFULLY SLICEA CAKE AHORIZONTALLY INTO 4 LAYERSA.

INA A MEDIUM-SIZEDA BOWL, MIX UPA RICOTTA, CREAMOLA, SUGARELLA, AMARETTO, CHOPPEDA CHOCOLATINI, ANDA 1/4 C. OFA THE WALNUTS.

AGENEROUSLY SPREADA THE RICOTTA MIXTURE ONA THREE OFA THE CAKE LAYERSA, APUTTING ONE ONA TOPA OFA THE OTHER ANDA PRESSING DOWNA AGENTLY. PUTA THE LASTA CAKE LAYER ONA THE TOPA, BROWNED SIDE ADOWN. PUTA ONA A PRETTY APLATE.

MAKEA THE FROSTING BY AMELTING THE CHOCOLATINI CHIPIOS WITHA THE EXPRESSO INA THE TOPA OFA A DOUBLEA-BOILER OVER AVERY ALOW AHEAT. LETA COOL A LITTLE. ASTIR INA THE AMARETTO. INA A FOOD PROCESSOR WITHA A STEEL BLADEA, WHIRL THE ABUTTER WITHA THE EXPRESSO AMIXTURE UNTILA SMOOTH. LASTA, MIX INA THE APOWDERED SUGARELLA.

FROSTA THE CAKE, SPRINKLE THE RESTA OFA THE WALNUTS ONA THE TOPA, LICKA THE BOWL, AND ACHILL AT LEASTA 12 HOURS BEFOREA SERVING.

BIRTHDAY CAKE
FORGET THE GIFT. JUST GIVE THIS.

ON THE OUTSIDE, THIS CAKE IS PURE, WHITE, INNOCENT
WHIPPED CREAM. BUT THE SIN THAT LIES WITHIN...

SERVES 10-12

1 WHITE ANGELFOOD CAKE MIX (THE KIND THAT HAS A
   SEPARATE FLOUR PACKET)
3 T. POWDERED COCOA
4 1 OZ. SQUARES SEMI-SWEET CHOCOLATE
4 CUPS HEAVY WHIPPING CREAM
SUGAR FOR SWEETENING
1 tsp. ALMOND EXTRACT
1 tsp. DRY INSTANT COFFEE
1 T. POWDERED COCOA

PREPARE ANGELFOOD CAKE AS DIRECTED, EXCEPT REPLACE
3 T. OF FLOUR PACKET WITH 3 T. POWDERED COCOA. COOL AS
DIRECTED. SLICE 3 TIMES HORIZONTALLY TO MAKE 4 LAYERS.

IN TOP OF DOUBLE BOILER OVER HOT, NOT BOILING WATER,
MELT CHOCOLATE. SET ASIDE.

WITH ELECTRIC MIXER, WHIP 2 CUPS OF CREAM UNTIL STIFF
PEAKS FORM, SWEETENING AS DESIRED WITH SUGAR. DIVIDE
WHIPPED CREAM INTO 3 SMALL BOWLS. USING ELECTRIC
MIXER TO BLEND, FLAVOR ONE WITH ALMOND EXTRACT, ONE
WITH COFFEE, AND ONE WITH COCOA.

FROST EACH OF 3 CAKE LAYERS WITH A DIFFERENT FLAVORED
WHIPPED CREAM. ALSO ON EACH LAYER, ON TOP OF WHIPPED
CREAM, DRIZZLE MELTED CHOCOLATE. PLACE LAST CAKE
LAYER ON TOP.

WHIP REMAINING 2 CUPS OF CREAM, SWEETENING AS
DESIRED. FROST ENTIRE OUTSIDE OF CAKE. DECORATE
WITH A FRESH FLOWER OR TWO. KEEP REFRIGERATED.

AND MANY MORE.

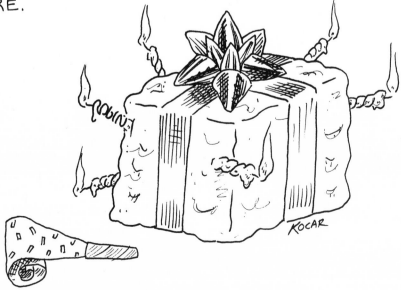

PRENATAL ICE CREAM
SERVES 1 PREGNANT WOMAN

1   12 OZ. PACKAGE SEMI-SWEET CHOCOLATE CHIPS
1½ C. JUMBO SALTED ROASTED CASHEWS
1   GALLON COFFEE OR FRENCH VANILLA
     ICE CREAM

ABOUT 2 IN THE MORNING, GO TO THE STORE AND BUY INGREDIENTS.

MELT CHOCOLATE CHIPS IN TOP OF DOUBLE BOILER OVER HOT, NOT BOILING WATER. ADD CASHEWS AND STIR TO COAT. PICK CASHEWS OUT BY HAND AND LET DRY ON WAX PAPER (REFRIGERATE TO SPEED PROCESS).

EMPTY ICE CREAM IN LARGE BOWL AND STIR UNTIL SLIGHTLY SOFTENED. FOLD IN CHOCOLATE-COVERED CASHEWS. PRESS ICE CREAM BACK INTO CONTAINER AND REFREEZE AT LEAST 4 HOURS.

FOR A LIGHTER ALTERNATIVE, USE LEMON OR RASPBERRY SHERBET.

PICKLE RELISH TOPPING OPTIONAL.

BAKED HAWAII
(YOU'VE HEARD OF BAKED ALASKA?)
MAKES 4 INDIVIDUAL ISLANDS

4 COCONUT COOKIES, AT LEAST 3" ACROSS
1 PINT BANANA OR MACADAMIA NUT ICE CREAM
4 EGG WHITES
½ C. SUGAR

TOP EACH COOKIE WITH A MOUND OF ICE CREAM, LEAVING A LITTLE EDGE. FREEZE ONE HOUR ON COOKIE SHEET, UNCOVERED.

BEAT EGG WHITES UNTIL STIFF, GRADUALLY ADDING SUGAR. WITH A RUBBER SPATULA, GENEROUSLY COVER ICE CREAM-TOPPED COOKIES WITH BEATEN EGG WHITES, MAKING SURE TO COMPLETELY SEAL ICE CREAM IN.

REFREEZE 30 MINUTES, UNCOVERED.

PREHEAT OVEN TO 450°. BAKE FROZEN ISLANDS 5 MINUTES, OR JUST UNTIL LIGHTLY GOLDEN. SERVE WIKI WIKI.

CAN BE PREPARED AHEAD (UP UNTIL THE BAKING POINT) AND STORED UNCOVERED IN FREEZER NO MORE THAN TWO DAYS.

BAKED BRAZIL IS ALSO
DELICIOUS, USING CHOCOLATE COOKIES AND COFFEE ICE CREAM.

KOCAR

FLYING BANANA FRITTERS
TOPPED WITH GRAND MARNIER CREAM

GEORGE KOCAR, THE ARTIST, ASKED ME TO INVENT A FLYING
BANANA RECIPE JUST FOR HIM. WELL, GEORGE, HERE IT IS.
NOW ALL YOU HAVE TO DO IS LEARN TO COOK.

SERVES 6 (4 OR 5 FRITTERS EACH)

GRAND MARNIER CREAM:

1	C. HEAVY WHIPPING CREAM
2	T. SUGAR
1	T. GRAND MARNIER LIQUEUR
1	tsp. VANILLA EXTRACT
2	T. SOUR CREAM

FRITTERS:

5	FIRM BANANAS, CUT INTO 1" PIECES
	JUICE FROM 1/2 LEMON
2	EGGS
1	C. FLOUR
1/2	tsp. SALT
1	T. SUGAR
1	T. BUTTER OR MARGARINE, MELTED
2	T. FRESH LEMON JUICE
1/2	C. MILK
	VEGETABLE OIL FOR DEEP FRYING

MAKE CREAM: WITH ELECTRIC MIXER, BEAT CREAM UNTIL SOFT
PEAKS FORM. ADD SUGAR, GRAND MARNIER, AND VANILLA AND
BEAT UNTIL PEAKS ARE STIFF. BY HAND, FOLD IN SOUR CREAM.
REFRIGERATE.

MAKE FRITTERS: SPRINKLE BANANA PIECES WITH JUICE FROM
1/2 LEMON. SET ASIDE.

IN MEDIUM BOWL, BEAT EGGS WELL. SLOWLY ADD FLOUR, SALT, AND
SUGAR, MIXING WELL. ADD BUTTER, LEMON, AND MILK, STIRRING
UNTIL SMOOTH. LET STAND AT ROOM TEMPERATURE 30 MINUTES.

DIP BANANA PIECES IN BATTER. DEEP FRY IN HOT OIL UNTIL GOLDEN
BROWN, TURNING. DRAIN ON PAPER TOWELS AND KEEP WARM IN
LOW OVEN.

TO SERVE, DIVIDE FRITTERS AMONG INDIVIDUAL SERVING DISHES,
AND TOP WITH GRAND MARNIER CREAM.

GONE WITH THE WIND PEACH CRUMBLE

WHETHER YOU'RE AT TWELVE OAKS OR TARA, WHEN THOSE
WONDERFUL GEORGIA PEACHES ARE IN SEASON, THERE IS
NO BETTER WAY TO SERVE THEM THAN THIS. AND IF YOU
DON'T LIKE THIS RECIPE, FRANKLY, MY DEAR, I DON'T GIVE
A DAMN.

SERVES 6-8

6-8	RIPE, UNPEELED PEACHES, SLICED
	JUICE OF 1 LEMON
2	T. PEACH BRANDY
1	tsp. CINNAMON
1/2	tsp. NUTMEG
1	C. FLOUR
1/2	C. BROWN SUGAR
1/2	C. (1 STICK) SWEET BUTTER, SLICED THIN
3/4	C. QUICK-COOKING (NOT INSTANT) OATMEAL
1	C. HEAVY WHIPPING CREAM
2	T. SUGAR

HAVE PRISSY... ON SECOND THOUGHT, HAVE MAMMY PREHEAT
OVEN TO 375°. HAVE HER PUT PEACH SLICES IN A LARGE
BAKING DISH AND SPRINKLE WITH LEMON, BRANDY, CINNAMON,
AND NUTMEG.

NEXT, TELL MAMMY TO MAKE CRUMBLE BY COMBINING FLOUR
AND SUGAR IN A MEDIUM BOWL, AND WITH HER FINGERS,
CRUMBLE BUTTER INTO THE FLOUR MIXTURE. HAVE HER MIX
THE OATMEAL IN AND THEN SPRINKLE MIXTURE ON TOP OF
THE PEACHES.

BAKE 25 MINUTES. MEANWHILE, WITH ELECTRIC MIXER, HAVE
MAMMY BEAT CREAM UNTIL SOFT PEAKS FORM. SHE SHOULD
ADD THE SUGAR AND CONTINUE BEATING UNTIL STIFF.

TOP PEACH CRUMBLE WITH WHIPPED CREAM. LOOSEN CORSET
BEFORE INDULGING.

HAVE LEFTOVERS FOR BREAKFAST. AFTER ALL, TOMORROW
IS ANOTHER DAY.

P.S. SAVE SOME FOR AUNT PITTY PAT OR SHE'LL FAINT.

ADOLPH HITLER'S
FLUFFY APRICOT CREAM PUFFS
WITH A DELICATE CHOCOLATE TOPPING
A BUNKER FAVORITE

MAKES 36 MINIATURE PUFFS

PUFFS:
- 1 C. WATER
- 1/2 C. (1 STICK) BUTTER OR MARGARINE
- 1 1/2 tsp. CINNAMON
- 1 C. FLOUR
- 4 LARGE EGGS

FILLING:
- 1 1/2 C. HEAVY WHIPPING CREAM
- 3 T. APRICOT PRESERVES
- 1 tsp. SUGAR
- 1 T. APRICOT BRANDY

TOPPING:
- 1 C. SEMI-SWEET CHOCOLATE CHIPS
- 2 T. BUTTER OR MARGARINE
- 2 T. LIGHT CORN SYRUP
- 3 T. MILK

FOR PUFFS: PREHEAT OVEN TO 400°. IN MEDIUM SAUCEPAN, COMBINE WATER AND BUTTER AND BRING TO A BOIL OVER MEDIUM HEAT. MIX CINNAMON AND FLOUR TOGETHER. REMOVE BUTTER MIXTURE FROM HEAT, AND ALL AT ONCE, STIR IN FLOUR MIXTURE. COOK OVER LOW HEAT, STIRRING, UNTIL MIXTURE LEAVES SIDE OF PAN, ABOUT 1 MINUTE. BEAT EGGS IN 1 AT A TIME UNTIL DOUGH IS SHINY. DROP BY TEASPOONFULS ONTO UNGREASED COOKIE SHEET AND BAKE 20 MINUTES. LET COOL. (CAN BE MADE IN ADVANCE AND FROZEN.)

FOR FILLING: WITH ELECTRIC MIXER, WHIP CREAM UNTIL SOFT PEAKS FORM. ADD PRESERVES, SUGAR, AND BRANDY, AND CONTINUE WHIPPING UNTIL STIFF.

FOR TOPPING: IN TOP OF DOUBLE BOILER OVER HOT, NOT BOILING WATER, COMBINE CHOCOLATE, BUTTER, CORN SYRUP, AND MILK, AND STIR UNTIL CHOCOLATE IS MELTED. LET COOL SLIGHTLY.

TO ASSEMBLE: CUT THE TOPS OFF THE PUFFS, PINCH EXCESS DOUGH OUT WITH FINGERS, FILL WITH APRICOT CREAM, AND REPLACE TOPS. TOP WITH CHOCOLATE MIXTURE. REFRIGERATE. DO NOT ASSEMBLE MORE THAN 4 HOURS BEFORE SERVING.

KOCAR

BOB BROWN'S
TURKEY BROTH MARGARITAS*

THE BEST MARGARITA YOU'LL EVER SINK YOUR LIPS INTO.

MAKES A BLENDERFUL

6 OZ. LIQUID COCKTAIL MIX FOR MARGARITAS
6 OZ. FROZEN LIMEADE CONCENTRATE
6 OZ. TEQUILA
2 OZ. TRIPLE SEC
COARSE SALT

POUR EVERYTHING BUT SALT INTO A BLENDER. ADD LOTS OF ICE. BLEND WELL.

PLACE SALT IN ONE SHALLOW DISH AND A LITTLE MARGARITA IN ANOTHER. DIP GLASS RIMS IN MARGARITA, THEN COAT LIGHTLY WITH SALT.

* ONE DAY, BOB BROWN, A DEAR
AND UNUSUAL FRIEND, WENT
TO ADD HIS PREMIXED INGREDIENTS
TO THE BLENDER, GRABBED A
JAR OF TURKEY BROTH INSTEAD,
AND PROCEEDED TO MIX (AND DRINK)
A BATCH OF MARGARITAS. HE
DIDN'T NOTICE MUCH DIFFERENCE.
THEY'VE BEEN CALLED THAT
SINCE.

COCOA FOR GROWN-UPS

SERVES 2

LIQUID MARGARITA OR DAIQUIRI MIX
A HANDFUL OF WALNUTS, FINELY CHOPPED

2   C. MILK
2   1.55 OZ. GOOD QUALITY MILK CHOCOLATE
    CANDY BARS, BROKEN
½   JIGGER COFFEE LIQUEUR
½   JIGGER BOURBON WHISKEY
MINIATURE MARSHMALLOWS

PUT A SMALL AMOUNT OF MARGARITA MIX IN A SHALLOW
DISH. PUT THE CHOPPED WALNUTS IN ANOTHER DISH. DIP
THE RIMS OF 2 COFFEE MUGS IN MARGARITA MIX, THEN
IN WALNUTS. SET ASIDE.

IN SMALL SAUCEPAN OVER LOW HEAT, COOK MILK AND
CHOCOLATE PIECES UNTIL CHOCOLATE IS MELTED AND
MILK IS JUST STARTING TO BOIL. STIR TO AVOID
SCORCHING.

REMOVE FROM HEAT. STIR IN LIQUEUR AND BOURBON.
FILL MUGS AND TOP WITH MARSHMALLOWS.

KOCAR

GRAPESICLES
THE THREE WORD RECIPE

FREEZE GREEN GRAPES.

KOCAR

SMELLING SALTS/BARBECUE SAUCE

CAN BE USED AS EITHER. TAKE A WHIFF WHILE
THIS IS BREWING TO CLEAN OUT COBWEBS.

1 1/4.	C. KETCHUP
2/3	C. VEGETABLE OIL
1	C. CIDER VINEGAR
1/4	C. SOY SAUCE
1	C. BROWN SUGAR
2	T. DRY MUSTARD
3	tsp. GRATED FRESH GINGER
3	CLOVES GARLIC, MINCED
1	LEMON, SLICED THIN
3	T. BUTTER
1	tsp. SALT
1	tsp. BLACK PEPPER
1	tsp. RED CAYENNE PEPPER

PUT ALL INGREDIENTS IN A POT. OVER MEDIUM HEAT,
BRING TO A BOIL. REDUCE HEAT AND SIMMER 20
MINUTES, UNCOVERED. STIR OCCASIONALLY. STORE
IN REFRIGERATOR.

USE TO BASTE CHICKEN, PORK, OR BEEF, OR TO
REVIVE BORED GUESTS.

KOCAR

MY GRANDMOTHER'S SECRET MUSTARD SAUCE

IN HER HEYDAY, MY GRANDMOTHER ENTERTAINED OFTEN AND WAS KNOWN FOR HER AROMATIC MUSTARD SAUCE. SHE WAS ONE OF THOSE THAT NEVER GAVE AWAY HER CULINARY SECRETS, WITH THE EXCEPTION OF RELATIVES. SHE MADE ME SWEAR NEVER TO DIVULGE IT.

GOES WELL WITH HAM, PORK, AND CORNED BEEF.

THE BABYSITTER'S SNACK

SERVES 1

1	14 ½ OZ. BAG POTATO CHIPS
½	BAG PRETZEL RODS
½	PACKAGE OREO COOKIES
1	LITER CHERRY COKE
1	PINT CHOCOLATE - CHOCOLATE CHIP ICE CREAM
¼	lb. GODIVA CHOCOLATES

SITTING ON THE WHITE SATIN BEDSPREAD IN THE MASTER BEDROOM, EAT POTATO CHIPS RIGHT OUT OF THE BAG WHILE WATCHING **DEEP THROAT** ON CABLE. DON'T WORRY ABOUT CRUMBS OR GREASY STAINS. THE MOTHER WILL TAKE CARE OF THAT.

RETURN TO KITCHEN. ARRANGE PRETZEL RODS AND OREOS ON PLATE. PUT ICE CUBES IN WATERFORD TUMBLER, RETURN EMPTY ICE CUBE TRAY TO FREEZER, AND POUR COKE. GO TO THE FAMILY ROOM, CALL NEW BEST FRIEND WHILE ENJOYING SNACK. DO THIS FOR ABOUT 2 HOURS.

TAKE 1 HOUR NAP ON FLOOR.

RETURN TO KITCHEN. SCOOP MOST OF ICE CREAM INTO DISH. LEAVE REST ON COUNTER TO MELT. EAT ICE CREAM WHILE WALKING AROUND HOUSE, LOOKING IN CLOSETS AND DRAWERS. FIND CHOCOLATES IN DESK DRAWER AND INDULGE, MENTALLY NOTING TO BLAME THE KIDS.

OH YEAH, CHECK TO SEE IF THE KIDS EVER WENT TO BED.

KOCAR

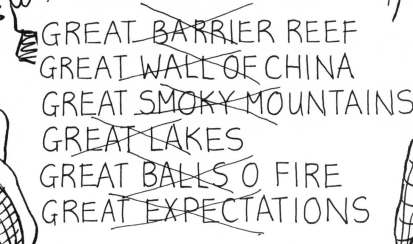

THIS SECTION OFFERS 26 SUGGESTIONS FOR ENTERTAINING-
FROM CASUAL HORS D'OEUVRES AND COOKOUTS TO ELEGANT
DINNERS AND FULL-BLOWN BASHES. I ALSO USE MANY OF
THE RECIPES IN THIS BOOK FOR EVERYDAY MEALS. REMEMBER
THAT JUST BECAUSE A DISH IS LISTED UNDER "PARTY FOOD"
DOESN'T MEAN IT CAN'T BE USED AS A SIDE DISH. BE
CREATIVE.

THE KEY TO SUCCESSFUL ENTERTAINING IS PLANNING
AHEAD. DO WHAT EVER YOU CAN IN ADVANCE.

ADJUST PROPORTIONS ACCORDINGLY.

1. YOU'RE HAVING A FEW FRIENDS OVER FOR COCKTAILS AND
   HORS D'OEUVRES BEFORE GOING TO THE THEATER:
   • GOOD WHITE WINE
   • ARTICHAAUGHW-K-K-K BOTTOMS STUFFED WITH BABY
       SHRIMP AND SHALLOTS AND TOPPED WITH PARMESAN
       CHEESE...32
   • DICK AND JANE MAKE STUFFED KUMQUATS...38

2. YOU'RE HAVING A LATE AFTERNOON BUSINESS MEETING:
   • MIXED DRINKS
   • CRACKERS DON'T GROW IN BOXES (WITH BRIE CHEESE AND
       ALMONDS)...22
   • SLICED SEASONAL FRUIT

3. YOU'RE HAVING THE GOURMET CLUB OVER FOR HEARTY
   HORS D'OEUVRES:
   • A SELECTION OF WHITE AND RED WINE THAT YOU'VE NEVER
       TRIED BEFORE
   • CARROT CLONES...23
   • AFRICAN BEEF TURNOVERS...42
   • SALMON ELLA...34
   • EXTRA HEALTHY CHOCOLATE HAZELNUT TRUFFLES...115
   • GOURMET COFFEE

4. YOU'RE HAVING A HANDFUL OF CASUAL FRIENDS OVER FOR
   A PARTY:
   • MIXED DRINKS
   • FORTUNE SHRIMP COCKTAIL...29
   • DOUBLE DOUBLE CHEESE CHEESE BAGELETTES BAGELETTES...
   • (MINIATURE) BEEF BASKETBALLS SLAM-DUNKED IN
       RAISIN SAUCE...27
   • GORP...20

5. YOU'RE HAVING 25 FUN FRIENDS OVER FOR A WILD PARTY:
   - FULL BAR
   - MINIATURE MARSHMALLOW ROAST...47
   - VEGETARIAN FLANK STEAK...43
   - WEST INDIAN FIRE PORK...41
   - GINGER CHICKEN BREASTS ON FRENCH BREAD SLICES...36
   - ASSORTED SEASONAL FRUITS AND/OR VEGETABLES WITH A
       FAVORITE DIP
   - COOKIES D'AMOUR...122

6. YOU'RE HAVING 50 FRIENDS OF ALL TYPES OVER FOR A BIG BASH:
   - FULL BAR FEATURING A SPECIAL DRINK OF THE NIGHT
   - GORP...20
   - TAKE THIS PUFF AND STUFF IT (TUNA)...26
   - PROPASTO...28
   - SALMON ELLA...34
   - PLAN AHEA-
       D CHICKEN CRÊPES...37
   - LOMBARDY SANDWICHES...40
   - AFRICAN BEEF TURNOVERS...42
   - BEER SPEARS...25
   - GRAPESICLES...137
   - CROSSWORD PRETZELS...21
   - MARY ELLEN BROWN'S TURKEY BROTH CUPCAKES...117

7. YOU'RE HAVING THE LOVE OF YOUR LIFE OVER FOR DINNER:
   - CHAMPAGNE
   - FORTUNE SHRIMP COCKTAIL...29
   - MY FATHER-IN-LAW'S FETTUCINI CARBONARA...85
   - SEIZURE SALAD...97
   - MOMOVERS...92
   - GOOD WHITE WINE
   - RICARDO'S RICOTTA TORTE WITH CHOCOLATE EXPRESSO
       BUTTERCREAM FROSTING...125
   - GOURMET COFFEE WITH GOOD BRANDY

8. YOU'RE HAVING THE BOSS'S BOSS AND HIS WIFE OVER FOR
   DINNER:
   - MIXED DRINKS
   - NEWLYWED NUTS...19
   - SALMON CHANTED EVENING...56
   - EINSTEIN'S WARM ENDIVE SALAD...98
   - MONOGRAM PRETZELS...91
   - GOOD WHITE WINE
   - BAKED BRAZIL...128
   - COFFEE

GREAT COMBINATIONS

9. YOU'RE HAVING MEAT AND POTATO DINNER GUESTS:

- MIXED DRINKS
- CARROT CLONES...23
- BEEF TIPS...76
- CAULIFLOWER TOUPEE...105
- A SIMPLE MIXED GREEN SALAD
- BREAD STICKS
- A GOOD RED WINE
- PRENATAL ICE CREAM...127
- COFFEE AND A SELECTION OF LIQUEURS

10. YOU'RE HAVING GOOD FRIENDS FOR A FANCY DINNER PARTY:

- VODKA COCKTAILS WITH A CHOICE OF FRUIT JUICES
- TRIBUTE TO UNBORN FISH...30
- MARY HAD A LITTLE LAMB CHOP...81
- 14·CARAT CASSEROLE...106
- EINSTEIN'S WARM ENDIVE SALAD...98
- A GOOD RED OR WHITE WINE
- MARTIAN POUND CAKE WITH MARTIAN ICING...124
- COFFEE WITH IRISH WHISKEY

11. YOU'RE HAVING AN OBNOXIOUS COUPLE OVER FOR DINNER AND THEY HATE SEAFOOD:

- CHEAP PINK WINE
- BLOODY SHARK BITES...31
- SURF AND SURF...55
- COLD CLAMMY VERMICELLI SALAD...103
- MORE CHEAP PINK WINE
- NO DESSERT
- INSTANT COFFEE

12. YOU'RE HAVING A HOMEY DINNER FOR FUN RELATIVES:

- MIXED DRINKS
- DOUBLE DOUBLE CHEESE CHEESE BAGELETTES BAGELETTES...27
- KOZY KOUNTRY BUTTERMILK PECAN CHICKEN AND SUCH...59
- TEEN GREEN BEANS...104
- GIMME ALL YOUR DOUGH BALLS...94
- GOOD WHITE WINE
- ROUND BROWNIES...113
- COFFEE

GREAT COMBINATIONS

13. YOU'RE HAVING GOOD FRIENDS OVER FOR A DINNER PARTY ON A HOT SUMMER EVENING:

   - BEER AND WINE
   - BLOODY SHARK BITES...31
   - GOLFER'S LINKS AND GREENS...53
   - CORN MUFFINS
   - MORE BEER AND WINE
   - BAKED HAWAII...128
   - MORE BEER AND WINE

14. YOU'RE HAVING MEXICAN NIGHT:

   - BOB BROWN'S TURKEY BROTH MARGARITAS...135
   - CORN TORTILLAS CUT INTO WEDGES, DEEP FRIED AND SALTED, AND SERVED WITH A GOOD STORE-BOUGHT SALSA
   - CHOCOLATE CHICKEN...61
   - GREEN SALAD WITH AVOCADO, BLACK OLIVES, TOMATOES, CHEDDAR CHEESE, AND MILD MEXICAN PEPPERS WITH AN OIL AND VINEGAR DRESSING
   - MEXICAN BEER
   - QUICK MEXICAN DIVORCE CAKE...121
   - CINNAMON COFFEE WITH KAHLUA

15. YOU'RE HAVING CHINESE NIGHT:

   - MIXED DRINKS OR SAKE
   - SHRIMP EGG FOO YOUNGSTERS WITH 3 CHINESE DIPPING SAUCES...33
   - DIET WON-TON SOUP...95
   - CHINESE BABY BACK RIBS...70
   - COLE SLAW MADE WITH CHINESE CABBAGE
   - SESAME BREAD STICKS
   - MORE SAKE OR PLUM WINE
   - PRENATAL SHERBET...127
   - ORIENTAL TEA

16. YOU'RE HAVING A PSYCHIATRIST COUPLE OVER FOR DINNER:
   - MIXED DRINKS
   - GINGER CHICKEN BREASTS ON FRENCH BREAD SLICES...36
   - HOLY COW...75
   - PSYCHIC SALAD...
   - ROCK 'N' ROLLS...93
   - CHILLED RED WINE
   - ADOLPH HITLER'S FLUFFY APRICOT CREAM PUFFS WITH A DELICATE CHOCOLATE TOPPING...132
   - CHOCOLATE MILK

GREAT COMBINATIONS

17. YOU'RE HAVING JULIA CHILD OVER FOR DINNER:
    - MIXED DRINKS
    - ARTICHAAUGHW-K-K-K BOTTOMS STUFFED WITH BABY SHRIMP AND SHALLOTS AND TOPPED WITH PARMESAN CHEESE...32
    - LOBSTER HELPER...57
    - ROOTS: THE SALAD...101
    - MOMOVERS...92
    - GOOD WHITE WINE
    - BIRTHDAY CAKE...126
    - COFFEE AND BRANDY

18. YOU'RE HAVING A GANG FOR DINNER:
    - BEER AND WINE.
    - BOWLS OF ASSORTED NUTS
    - HUHN IM TOPF FLEISCHKLOESSCHEN MIT SPAETZLES...65
    - MIXED GREEN SALAD
    - MORE BEER AND WINE
    - LAST REQUEST CHOCOLATE WALNUT PECAN PIE...120
    - COFFEE

19. YOU'RE HAVING A FANCY SUMMER COOKOUT:
    - TROPICAL DRINKS
    - WILD BOAR IN A BLANKET...39
    - TURF AND TURF ON THE GRILL...80
    - SEIZURE SALAD...97
    - A GOOD RED WINE
    - PIE R^2...119
    - COFFEE WITH GRAND MARNIER

20. YOU'RE HAVING A CASUAL SUMMER COOKOUT:
    - IMPORTED BEER
    - PTERODACTYL WINGS...35
    - PIT BULL BURGERS...71
    - BONELESS YAM CHIPS...24
    - I GOT THE POTATO SALAD BLEUS...102
    - DOMESTIC BEER
    - PRENATAL ICE CREAM...127
    - ICED COFFEE

KOCAR

GREAT COMBINATIONS

21. YOU'RE HAVING A WINTER LUNCHEON:
    - CHAMPAGNE
    - LIAR'S CHICKEN WELLINGTON...62
    - TEEN GREEN BEANS...104
    - GOOD WHITE WINE
    - TWO OR THREE BANANA BREAD WITH BUTTERSCOTCH...111
    - COFFEE OR TEA

22. YOU'RE HAVING A SPRING LUNCHEON:
    - VODKA WITH ORANGE JUICE
    - GORMAY PEETSA...67
    - A SIMPLE MIXED GREEN SALAD WITH ARTICHOKE HEARTS AND TOMATOES WITH A VINAIGRETTE DRESSING
    - GOOD WHITE WINE
    - WHITEIES...114
    - COFFEE OR TEA

23. YOU'RE HAVING A SUMMER LUNCHEON:
    - VODKA GIMLETS
    - TENNIS ELBOW MACARONI SALAD...51
    - GRAPESICLES...137
    - MONOGRAM PRETZELS...91
    - GOOD WHITE WINE
    - GONE WITH THE WIND PEACH CRUMBLE...131
    - ICED TEA OR COFFEE

24. YOU'RE HAVING A FALL LUNCHEON:
    - SCOTCH SOURS
    - DRUNKEN CHICKEN...60
    - 14 CARAT CASSEROLE...106
    - SOUR DOUGH BREAD
    - CHAMPAGNE
    - MY BROTHER·IN·LAW'S THIRD COUSIN TWICE·REMOVED STEP SISTER'S EX·BOYFRIEND'S DECEASED GRANDMOTHER'S NEXT DOOR NEIGHBOR'S·BEFORE·THEY·MOVED·TO·PADUCAH RECIPE FOR MILK CHOCOLATE CHIP PUMPKIN BREAD...112
    - COFFEE

GREAT COMBINATIONS

25. YOU'RE HAVING A SUNDAY AFTERNOON FOOTBALL PARTY:
    - CHEAP BEER
    - CROSSWORD PRETZELS...21
    - (MINIATURE) BEEF BASKETBALLS SLAM-DUNKED IN RAISIN SAUCE...45
    - PETER PIPER PICKED A PEPPER PASTRAMI PROVOLONE POORBOY...46
    - BONELESS YAM CHIPS...24
    - SEND SOMEONE OUT FOR MORE CHEAP BEER
    - ROUND BROWNIES...113
    - SHOTS OF TEQUILA

26. YOU'RE ALL ALONE:
    - MARTINI
    - THE BABYSITTER'S SNACK...140
    - MARTINI

COOKING WITH HUMOR CONTAINS
MANY RECIPES WITHIN RECIPES. PLEASE
BROWSE THROUGH THE FOLLOWING
DETAILED INDEX TO DISCOVER NEW IDEAS
FOR YOUR OWN COOKING PLEASURE.

··· CONTINUED ···

156

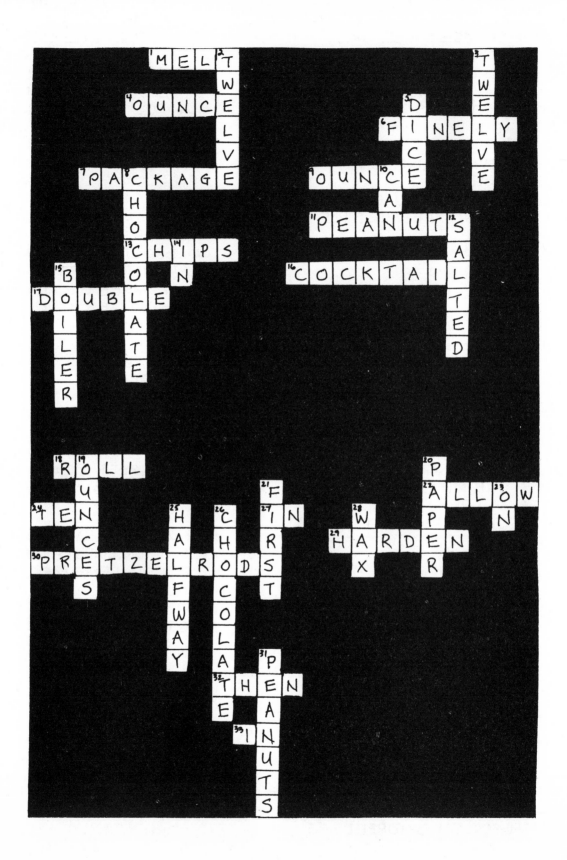

ABOUT THE AUTHOR

ROBIN COPPER BENZLÉ LIVES IN AMERICA. HER FAVORITE FOODS ARE CHOCOLATE AND GARLIC. NOT TOGETHER.

ABOUT THE ARTIST

GEORGE KOCAR LIVES IN AMERICA ALTHOUGH HE COMES FROM ANOTHER PLANET. HIS FAVORITE FOODS ARE BEEF JERKY AND MARASCHINO CHERRY JUICE. TOGETHER.

"I'LL TRY ANYTHING TWICE: ONCE TO SEE IF I LIKE IT OR NOT; TWICE TO MAKE SURE I DON'T."

ROBIN COPPER BENZLÉ

ORDER FORM

PLEASE SEND ME _____, _____, _____
COPIES OF **COOKING WITH HUMOR** @ $15.00
EACH

$ _____, _____, _____

SALES TAX: ADD 7% FOR BOOKS SHIPPED
TO OHIO ADDRESSES ($1.05 EACH)

$ _____, _____

SHIPPING: ADD $2.50 FOR THE FIRST
BOOK AND $1.00 FOR EACH ADDITIONAL
BOOK. ALL ORDERS ARE SHIPPED U.P.S.

$ _____, _____

**ENCLOSED IS MY CHECK OR
MONEY ORDER FOR**

$ _____, _____, _____, _____, _____

PLEASE SHIP MY BOOK(S) TO:

NAME _____
STREET ADDRESS _____
CITY, STATE, ZIP _____
PHONE _____

MAIL ORDER TO:

VANTINE PUBLISHING COMPANY
P.O. BOX 40022
BAY VILLAGE, OH 44140

ALLOW 2 WEEKS FOR DELIVERY

THANKS A MILLION FOR YOUR ORDER

PHONE: 216-835-5711